JOHN DEERE

Landscaping & Lawn Care

THE COMPLETE GUIDE TO A BEAUTIFUL YARD YEAR-ROUND

QUARRY

JOHN DEERE

Landscaping & Lawn Care

THE COMPLETE GUIDE TO A BEAUTIFUL YARD YEAR-ROUND

GLOUCESTER MASSACHUSETTS

QUARRY BOOKS

KRISTEN HAMPSHIRE

First published in the United States of America by
Quarry Books, a member of
Quayside Publishing Group
33 Commercial Street
Gloucester, Massachusetts 01930-5089
Telephone: (978) 282-9590
Fax: (978) 283-2742
www.quarrybooks.com

Library of Congress Cataloging-in-Publication Data
Hampshire, Kristen.
  John Deere's landscaping and lawn care : the complete guide to a beautiful yard year-round / Kristen Hampshire.
    p.   cm.
  ISBN 1-59253-343-4 (pbk.)
  1. Lawns. I. Title.
SB433.H285 2007
635.9'647—dc22   2007003099
                                                        CIP

ISBN-13: 978-1-59253-343-5
ISBN-10: 1-59253-343-4

10 9 8 7 6 5 4 3 2 1

Design: John Hall Design Group, www.johnhalldesign.com
Cover Image: Clive Nichols Garden Pictures/www.clivenichols.com
Illustrations by: Mario Ferro

Printed in USA

Contents

Go Outside and Play!

The time you dedicate to lawn care is an investment in your landscape and certainly a boon to property value. Mowing, watering, and fertilizing: these are the building blocks to a beautiful lawn. But what drives many of us outdoors isn't these tasks—it's the feeling we get while doing them. Yard work is a breath of fresh air. Drinking in the sweet fragrances of your flowers lifts the spirit, and the smell of fresh grass clippings signals spring. Hands-on activities and even routine maintenance provide a mental time-out from the hustle and bustle of our daily lives.

Ultimately, improving our surroundings delivers a sense of pride and purpose. Your hard labor produces results you can see and enjoy, so you begin to consider ways to improve your outdoor space, adding features that make it more livable, more *you*. After all, your yard is much more than a patch of grass. It is a canvas, a patchwork of nature reserved for your pleasure. What you make of it is your choice.

Whether you have a cozy plot or a few acres to play with, you'll find in this comprehensive guide the care notes and equipment suggestions you need to get started and to sharpen your skills. Learn tricks that professionals know, and put them to use in your landscape in no time. Expert advice from John Deere will get you going in the right direction.

The following pages are packed with cultivation instructions, project clinics, equipment how-tos, and design ideas. Quick Tips are sprinkled throughout chapters, so key information is easy to digest. We understand that our lawn care pursuits are often on the clock, so we give you the option to gobble up need-to-know details in a hurry.

Ready to vamp up your curb appeal? Try one of our Weekend Workshops (page 102), and gradually turn your backyard into an outdoor living room. High-impact features—such as ponds, pathways, and attractive landscape lighting—are all within reach, affording a luxury look without breaking the bank or taking a long time to complete. Inspiring photographs will spark your creativity, and nuts-and-bolts information on choosing the right equipment for each job ensures that you don't dig into a project unprepared.

So, get inspired—go outside and play! There's plenty in store for you here, so you can establish the landscape you always wanted.

A WELL-MAINTAINED YARD becomes a playground, a resting place, and an escape from the daily routine.

PART ONE

From the Ground Up

Hard-working grass prevents soil from eroding, absorbs pollution, and produces oxygen; it lives, breathes, and survives—if we treat it properly. Unfortunately, there is no such thing as a magic grass seed that will sprout effortlessly into emerald perfection.

Establishing an enviable lawn starts with the gardener's rule of thumb: Put the right plant in the right place. By knowing how turfgrass grows and what types of grasses will thrive on your property, you're one step closer to laying down the foundation of your outdoor living room.

CHAPTER 1

Turf Basics

Grass is stubborn—it has staying power. Every day, we test its ability to thrive under stressful conditions: our children trampling across its surface and treating it like an outdoor playroom; our pets rooting around and digging through the thick green, sometimes marking territory. Turfgrass withstands the burden of foot traffic, heavy equipment, and nature's climatic whims. But it has needs.

Establishing healthy grass begins with a biology lesson and includes a bit of science—agronomy. But by learning how grass grows, and under what conditions it thrives, you can stack the odds in your favor and enjoy a beautiful lawn.

If you think about it, grass crops up almost everywhere you look. It grows untamed in prairies, and it covers rocks in mosslike blankets. Even in desertscape regions, such as the Southwest, tufts of straw-textured, sun-dried grass cling to the sandy soil. In urban environments, you have probably noticed it peering through sidewalk cracks and claiming undeveloped lots. The grass in your front and backyard is intentional, an element of outdoor décor, the foundation for a landscape. But it is native to, and grows wild in, every zone of the world.

There are more than 75,000 different species of grass, and they include plants such as corn, sorghum, and bamboo. Under modern standards, you wouldn't define most of these varieties as grass. That's because our lofty expectations for what the grass on our properties should look like revolve around appearance. We want year-round green, indestructible green. If we could have our wish, we'd want our grass to be maintenance free: to mow, water, and fertilize itself. However, achieving curb appeal doesn't happen by itself—we have to work at it. The first step is choosing the right turfgrass for your location.

Roughly seventy-five of those 75,000 grass varieties are capable of withstanding repeated grazing or, in our case, mowing. And only half of those grasses are species you would want to grow in your lawn. For example, crabgrass and quackgrass don't grow into nice, dense turf. They look scrappy and weedy. These invasive grasses usually take over a lawn if proper turf care practices are neglected. Another important point: there is grass, and there is *turf*grass. The latter's growth habits and tolerance to stress—from climate to foot traffic—are the characteristics that help establish an attractive lawn.

The good news is that nature has done quite a bit of research for us. After generations of natural selection, turfgrasses that sustained over time can hold their own. Thanks to breeding and development of new cultivars, we have tweaked varieties to look greener, stand up to repeated mowing, and take root quickly. That leaves us today with a collection of cool- and warm-season grasses appropriate for various regions and climates.

Turfgrass Anatomy

Before we get into turfgrass varieties and choosing the right plant for your zone, let's zoom in on the key features—or body parts—that turfgrasses share: a crown, roots, shoots, rhizomes, stolons, and leaves. Based on the characteristics of these parts, turfgrass professionals can identify one variety from the next. Overall turfgrass quality is generally judged by a combination of color, leaf width, texture, and density.

Although we cover only a condensed turf science lesson here, an overview of the anatomy of turfgrass will help you understand how your lawn grows.

The main parts of a grass plant include the following:

Crown: Think of the crown as Grand Central for growth. It is the foundation of the plant from which roots and new leaves originate. Even if you shave the top growth off grass blades, and the roots suffer from poor soil and shrivel up, your grass has a fighting chance if the crown is intact. That is because roots and shoots emerge from the crown.

Roots: Fibrous root systems vary with turfgrass variety. For example, the roots of drought-tolerant species reach deep into the ground, so they can access as much moisture and as many nutrients as possible. Root density, depth, distribution, and contact to soil all have an influence on water absorption.

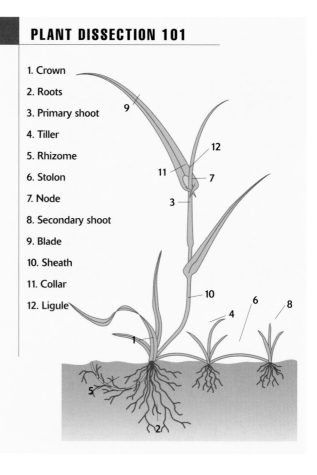

PLANT DISSECTION 101

1. Crown
2. Roots
3. Primary shoot
4. Tiller
5. Rhizome
6. Stolon
7. Node
8. Secondary shoot
9. Blade
10. Sheath
11. Collar
12. Ligule

Shoots: This is a general term that refers to growth that extends upward from the crown. *Primary shoots* develop first from the seed. *Tillers* are secondary shoots that develop from the crown. While all grasses form tillers, tall fescue is the most noted bunch grass, which grows in tufts, rather than spreading.

Rhizomes, Stolons, and Nodes: *Rhizomes* are below-ground stems that can sprout secondary shoots. *Stolons*, or runners, travel just above the surface and can also produce new plants. *Nodes* are a lot like joints. Each time a node on a stolon or rhizome sprouts, a *secondary shoot* develops roots. This spreading action is how creeping grasses grow. Bermuda grass and zoysia grass are two examples.

Leaf: Leaves develop from shoots and are composed of *blades* and *sheaths*. Blades are the broad upper portion, and sheaths wrap around the stem. The blade and sheath meet at the *collar*. Inside the collar is the *ligule*, which is a thin membrane or band of hairs. An extension of the collar is the *auricle*, which resembles an ear, as its name indicates.

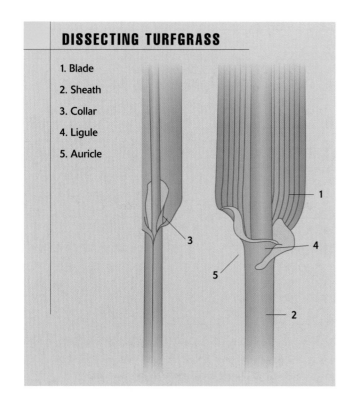

DISSECTING TURFGRASS

1. Blade
2. Sheath
3. Collar
4. Ligule
5. Auricle

Season Select: Warm or Cool?

Turfgrasses are divided into warm- and cool-season species. Cool-season grasses originated in Europe and North America. They can withstand winter weather, and they do not appreciate extreme heat. Their prime growth times are fall and spring. They thrive in temperatures between 60 and 75 degrees Fahrenheit (15° and 24°C). The texture of cool-season grass depends on the variety. While coarse tall fescue has thick blades, bluegrass has narrow, fine leaves.

Warm-season grasses are native to Africa, the Caribbean, the Bahamas—places in which you might vacation. They prefer southern climates and might hibernate during the winter chill. They grow best in temperatures between 80 and 95 degrees Fahrenheit (27° and 35°C).

Warm-season grasses fall into two types: savannah-type species and tropical grasses. Savannah grasses have narrower leaf blades than many warm-season species. A photosynthetic apparatus allows savannah grasses to survive warm, dry weather. You might find savanna varieties, such as Bermuda grass, growing in cities such as Phoenix, Arizona.

KENTUCKY BLUEGRASS is a hardy variety in the cool-season turfgrass family.

Tropical grasses, such as St. Augustine grass, behave quite differently. Native to humid climates, such as Florida, tropical grasses never developed a water conservation mechanism. Their leaf blades are broad, and the turf has a dense, almost bristly, texture.

Because warm- and cool-season grasses experience different peak-growth times, their care schedules vary. This is important to note because you should plan planting, aeration, fertilization, and any stressful activity during the time when the grass will recover the fastest. If you have cool-season grass, this means adding aeration, planting, and fertilization to your fall checklist. (For more seasonal care tips, refer to Appendix II on page 158.)

When planting, cool-season grasses should be seeded; warm-season grasses can be either sodded or *sprigged*, a method in which clippings from existing perennial grasses are replanted at the rooted nodes. Sprigging is generally used for warm-season grasses because they do not produce fertile seed; however, some seed is now available for select warm-season grasses.

ST. AUGUSTINE GRASS thrives in warm climates.

FALL SEEDING

ALLOW COOL-SEASON TURFSEED as much time as possible to establish and grow strong before the stressful summer. The prime season for planting cool-season grasses is fall, when there is less weed pressure. Just be sure to plan enough time for the seeds to sprout before the first hard frost. Otherwise, water in the seed will act like a frozen pipe, freezing, bursting, and ultimately killing the seed. Plant cool-season seed in September, so the plant will mature enough to withstand the winter.

Perennial or Annual Grasses?

Turfgrasses are also divided into categories based on whether they are annuals or perennials. Consider the difference between impatiens and daylilies, two popular garden flowers. Every year, you must purchase impatiens and plant them. They are single-season bloomers. Annual turfgrasses are much the same. Their biological clocks are regulated by air temperature and day length. The warmth of spring tells annual grasses it's time to sprout, and cooler autumn days signal winter hibernation, when annual turfgrasses die and disperse seed for the next year's growth. Their lifecycles in constant motion, they produce roots quickly and fill in fast. For this reason, annual grasses are often used in new construction, where preventing soil erosion and obtaining instant curb appeal is a priority. Contractors can count on annual grasses to sprout fast and cover the ground.

Unlike annual grasses, perennials do not die back in the fall. Long-term growers, perennial turfgrasses take longer to become established, but they can live for years and, in most cases, are the best choice for your lawn, because they are hardy and long lasting. If your lawn is mature, the turfgrass is most likely a perennial variety or a mix that includes annual and perennial grasses.

EACH SPRIG IS A GRASS PLANT, complete with leaf blades and roots. Sprinkle them across the area to be planted, and within a few months, they will spread by sending out runners. Water in the spring, just as you would seed: frequent, light watering to keep the soil constantly moist.

Zone in on Your Climate

You wouldn't plant a delicate rose in a desert and expect it to flourish, and planting a cactus on the coast would shock the drought-loving plant. Following the right-plant-in-the-right-place rule is just as important for turfgrass. Temperature, precipitation, humidity, and growing season affect turfgrass performance and survival. Choosing the best grass for your yard will depend on where you live. Not sure what to plant? The Turfgrass Climate Zone Map is a useful reference. The map divides the United States into various zones, based on how turfgrasses perform. This map differs from the USDA Plant Hardiness Zone Map because turfgrasses thrive in a greater range of temperatures than flowers and other plants. Climate maps are also available for Europe and the rest of the world.

To confuse matters, there are several versions of the Turfgrass Climate Zone Map. Some show seven zones; others show five. Some maps separate Florida and the Gulf Coast to create an eighth tropical zone. Seed companies develop their own maps to help customers purchase the right product, and maps that break down turfgrass zones by county are often available from state agricultural university extensions. A reliable general guide is the Turfgrass Climate Zone Map from the United States National Arboretum, which adapts and simplifies the USDA Plant Hardiness Zone Map into five zones.

Warm/Humid Zone

Insects and moisture-related diseases love this climate, so a regular lawn-care maintenance program is especially important for turf health. (Learn more in Chapter 7.) Soil is saturated, and turfgrasses in this area of the country go dormant for a few months during the winter, even when weather is mild. Bermuda grass is a common species here, as are St. Augustine grass and zoysia grass.

Cool/Humid Zone

This large area spans the top-right quarter of the United States, where typically long winters and milder summers create a roller-coaster environment for turfgrass. It must tolerate deep freezes, snow, and low temperatures and, in some states, very hot summers. Cool-season grasses, such as Kentucky bluegrass, are popular here.

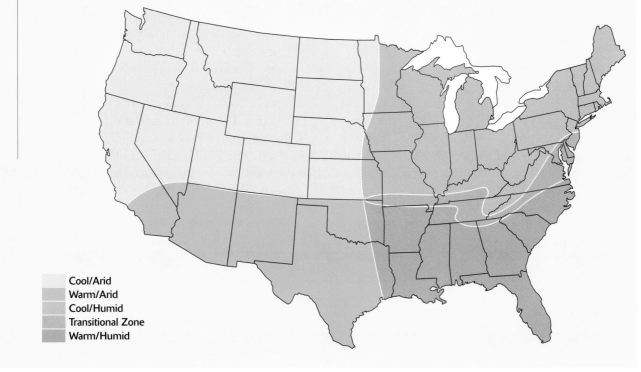

TURFGRASS CLIMATE ZONE MAP

CONSULT THIS MAP to get a general idea of the grasses that will thrive in your location. University agricultural extensions generally draw up specific state zone maps, which are much more detailed. These maps are especially helpful if you live in a transition zone state, such as North Carolina.

Cool/Arid
Warm/Arid
Cool/Humid
Transitional Zone
Warm/Humid

Knowing your climate zone will help you determine what type of turfgrass is best suited for your property and how you should care for it. For example, if you live in the warm and humid zone, your lawn-care responsibilities may persist through seasonable winter months.

Warm/Arid Zone

The arid Southwest hosts unique climate challenges for turfgrass. Certain areas can go weeks without rainfall, and water supply is generally a concern. Some communities even designate days on which homeowners may water their lawns, with conservation top of mind. Turfgrasses that perform best in this desert region dig their roots deep into the soil to drink up all available water. Warm-season grasses, such as Bermuda grass, grow in this zone. Warm-season grasses thrive only with proper irrigation.

Cool/Arid Zone

This zone spans an area with a variety of weather patterns. Temperatures can get quite cool in the northern half of this region, where you'll find mountaintops capped with snow. Other areas in this zone have more in common with the warm/arid zone and its desertscape. Meanwhile, the Plains states grow wild, prairie grasses—although in developed areas in this region, you'll find lush lawns. Because of the range in climate in this zone, it's a good idea to contact your state university agricultural extension for planting recommendations.

Transitional Zone

The transitional zone—where the climate isn't definitively warm or cool—is an area roughly 100 miles (161 km) on either side of a line drawn from Washington, D.C., through Cincinnati to St. Louis. Summers are too warm for cool-season grasses, and winters are too harsh for warm-season varieties. Growing grass is a challenge here. What do to? If you live north of Interstate 80, cool-season grasses, such as bluegrasses and ryegrasses, are a resilient option. If you live south of this line, but temperatures are cooler in winter, you'll want to plant warm-season grasses with some cold tolerance, such as Bermuda grass. Tall fescues can grow well in some states—North Carolina, for example—but will not perform if temperatures drop too low.

European Zones

The cool, marine climate in Great Britain, Scotland, and Ireland is known for its misty rain and fairly mild winters. Cool-season grasses love this weather; the consistently moist soil is comparable to the ideal irrigation system and provides a happy environment for plants. Continental Europe's cool winter temperatures also cater well to cool-season varieties.

Your Very Own Microclimate

A turfgrass climate map can help determine if your weather will accommodate cool- or warm-season grasses, but conditions close to home can have a strong impact on your grass-growing success. That stately evergreen tree provides year-round shade for a portion of your lawn, and the slope in your backyard sends water to the neighbor's property. Your southwest-facing flowerbed gets full sun in late afternoon, but the pergola over your patio covers potted plants from direct rays. Your property is a microclimate. Each tree and topographical nuance affects how turfgrass will perform.

So, how well do you know your microclimate?

Survey your property. Note where the turf is shaded by trees. Do these spots require less watering? Check out your lawn's curves. Are there swampy areas where the land is lower? Do you see brown patches on downhill slopes? The lay of the land affects water distribution. Take note of these factors before planting turfgrass or developing a lawn care program, and discuss your observations with a professional at a home and garden store or a landscape contractor. (See Appendix I for tips on hiring a professional.)

You can change some of your landscape conditions. Grading levels land, and thinning out evergreen tree canopies allows more sunlight to reach deprived turf. You can also choose plant varieties that thrive in full sun. These are a few examples, and a professional or university extension service will have other ideas for you.

Starting from Scratch

If you are reestablishing your lawn or moving into new construction with virgin soil, choose a high-quality turfgrass that will produce a thick, green lawn. You may not have actively considered the specific characteristics that separate a great-looking lawn from a basic yard, but a great-looking lawn starts with the seed you choose. Consider your microclimate, your lifestyle, and your maintenance expectations before making a choice. Some turfgrass varieties require more watering and protection against weed and disease than others. Here are some more things to keep in mind.

Traffic Tolerance: Children and dogs wear down turf, as does frequent mowing. The result is compaction and leaf blade damage. You want turf with strong roots and an ability to regenerate quickly. Dense lawns recover more quickly from damage, grow in faster, and generally look more attractive.

Emerald Green: Not every turfgrass is a rich shade of green. Species vary in color from light green to blue-green and Kelly green. Color is also an important consideration when patching a dead spot. You don't want to purchase a variety that grows in lime green if the rest of your lawn is Kentucky bluegrass.

Texture: If you've ever walked barefoot across a suburban lawn in Florida, you'll have noticed that the leaf blades are stiff, not soft and squishy, under your toes. This is because the warm-season grasses that thrive there have wider blades.

Drought and Disease Resistance: Some plants are more sensitive than others; they're more susceptible to insect infestation and less capable of fending off disease. While a solid lawn-care program—fertilization plus weed, disease, and insect prevention—will strengthen turfgrass, you don't want to start with a weak foundation. Each year, seed companies improve cultivars and introduce new ones. Find out which turfgrasses are peak performers by consulting with an expert at a nearby university extension service.

Seed or Sod?

You can establish a brand-new lawn in several ways—the best method for you depends on your patience, budget, and plant-care comfort level. The two most popular options are seeding and sodding. Seeding is, by far, the more economical choice, and you'll notice that many contractors who sod the front yards of new construction (for instant curb appeal) will plant seed at the sides and back. This is partly because of the price of sod and partly due to the need for instant erosion control. Growing grass from seed takes time and diligence, however, and is far less goof-proof than sod.

Whether you install sod or plant seed, be aware of the peak growth time for your turf variety. If you are planting cool-season turf, for example, you'll want to plan your project for the fall.

PROS AND CONS OF SEED AND SOD

SEED

PROS:
- More available turfgrass varieties
- Cost effective
- Convenient for fixing dead spots

CONS:
- Requires regular watering for up to three weeks, depending on the variety
- Can be difficult to spread seed at the correct rate
- Can take months before dense and attractive

SOD

PROS:
- Instant gratification
- Immediately prevents erosion
- Fast, relatively goof-proof installation

CONS:
- Costs as much as ten times more than seed
- A perishable crop, it must be lifted and laid within twenty-four hours of harvest from the sod farm
- Should be purchased as close to the production field as possible, so it can be transported and installed quickly, before sod roots dry out
- Is heavy and requires hard labor to transport and unload; this is best left to a professional

Planting Seed

There are a few mistakes most novice planters make that can sabotage a seeding project, and, because we do not plant turfgrass each year, 99.9 percent of us could use some pointers. The fraction of the population that has planting down to a science probably does it for a living. That said, you may opt to hire a landscape professional to install your new lawn. This is not a bad idea if you do not have the equipment, time, or patience to plant seed—and doing it properly requires all three of these things.

Where most homeowners go wrong when planting seed is with spreading. We purchase a 30-pound (13.6-kg) bag of seed on sale (another mistake we'll discuss later), we size up our bare property, and we begin walking rows up and down the property, throwing seed as if we are feeding a flock of starved birds.

Mistake Number One: Seed Overdose

Seeds need breathing room to sprout into seedlings, and they need their own territory to develop into plants. When we pour seeds on soil, figuring that the more we put down, the better our odds are of growing lots of grass, we really end up cramping the seeds. They choke each other, competing for water and nutrients. Many do not sprout at all, and those that do are not as strong because they have to share limited resources with so many seedlings. Their roots don't have enough room to develop more completely.

To avoid seed overdose, measure how much seed you need apply to your property. There are a couple of ways to do this. First, read the package. Then measure your lawn area by using a measuring wheel device or walking off the distance. (You can simply count steps and do the math to figure out the size of your lawn.) Distribute only the recommended amount of seed, generally 6 to 10 pounds (2.7 to 4.5 kg) per 1000 square feet (92.9 m²). If you are using a spreader to distribute seed, set your calibrator according to the seed producer's recommendations. If you are spreading seed by hand, figure out how much of the bag you should use up on your property, then pace yourself. For example, if you buy a 30-pound (13.6-kg) bag of seed and your property is 10,000 square feet (930 m²), you should only use up one-third of the bag. The best way to ensure even distribution is to spread half the rate in two rounds. Make one pass left to right across your lawn; make the next pass perpendicular.

USE A SPREADER to apply seed to the planting area.

Now, let's talk about what's in that bag. Did you buy a biggie-sized bag of seed from a sale display? Is it labeled Contractor's Mix or Kentucky 31? Does the label list a slew of turfgrass names? If you answered yes to all three of these questions, you've got trouble. You're most likely buying a low-grade turfseed that was designed to fill in fast. Unfortunately, it won't look as attractive or last as long as turfgrass from quality seed.

The eye-catching display of seed on sale at your local retailer may be the best buy, but if you don't read labels carefully, your planting efforts could go to waste on sub-par varieties. The following are some clues to help you determine what's really in the bag:

Trade Names: Beware of generic variety names, such as Kentucky bluegrass or perennial ryegrass. Better varieties earn patents under the Federal Plant Variety Protection Act, so pick seed with specific names, such as Best Planting Kentucky Bluegrass or Forever Fine Fescue. (These are fictitious names, but you get the idea.)

Seed Test Date: Check the label to find out which month and year the seed was produced. Some states require that bags be retested and relabeled after nine months to one year if not sold.

Vital Stats: Note also on the packaging the name of the producer/distributor, where the seed was grown, the lot number, and when the seed was tested.

After you spread the seed, lay down either a paper mulch product or straw. These materials decompose into the soil over time. They protect seeds from the scorching sun and help the soil retain moisture, which seeds desperately need to survive.

Mistake Number Two: Water Deprivation

Seeds are thirsty all the time. They need regular watering, and they depend on rainfall or you for water. Since it won't rain every day, you're on call. Once seed germination begins, the process is irreversible. If seeds dry out after germination, they could die from desiccation, although usually their growth will just be delayed. For the first two to three weeks of a seed's life, you must keep the top ¼ inch (6 mm) of soil moist. You can do this with sprinklers or an in-ground irrigation system, if you have one. Just be careful that you don't trample on freshly seeded ground to adjust sprinklers. Soil compaction from your footprints could damage the tender seedlings.

Many of us are impatient. We'll water a newly seeded lawn for a week, maybe two. But the thrill often wears off during week three, when seeds still need care and attention. Seeding is not difficult, but it is frustrating for many of us because we neglect the second half of the care schedule and wonder why we don't see a green carpet after all our efforts. Nature doesn't observe rush hour; plants develop gradually and mature over time. There is nothing we can do to make those little seeds sprout faster. Just water them consistently and treat them carefully.

High Germination: Check the germination percentage; the higher the number, the better chance the seed has of growing into a grass plant. Obviously, you want grass seed with the best odds possible.

Low Inert Matter: Broken seed and fillers are known as inert matter—substances that will not grow into a turfgrass plant. The lower the percentage of inert matter, the better.

Weed Seed Weight: Removing every weed seed during the cleaning process is next to impossible. Your seed blend will contain some of it, but choose a variety with weed seed weights between 0.3 and 0.5 percent.

No Noxious Weeds: If the bag label does not read: "Noxious Weeds: NONE FOUND," do not purchase it. Why take the chance of growing undesirable weeds?

Q: What is in contractor's mix seed? I often see this reference on bags at the store.

A: A contractor's main concern is to grow grass as fast as possible so that the soil doesn't wash away. Erosion control and fast establishment are the goals. Contractor's mix seed contains annual ryegrass, perennial ryegrass, and older, forage-type, tall fescue varieties—a collection of species. Annual ryegrass germinates in seven days, and forage-type grasses fill in quickly. What you sacrifice is quality. The grass is unattractive and designed as a crutch until homeowners replant. Annual ryegrass is also generally dirt cheap, making it an economical option.

We'll talk more about watering in Chapter 3, but for now, it's important to know that seeds like to be watered frequently, not deeply. In other words, water should have a chance to be absorbed by the soil, and the soil should always be moist. This even watering is critical. If you water too much, air won't reach the roots and they will rot. If you don't water enough, the seeds won't sprout.

Roll Out the Green Carpet

Sod is a great invention for those of us who want instant green—forget the seeds and the waiting period. Lay it down green side up, and you're in business—sort of. You must prepare the soil so the sod roots establish themselves effectively. Before laying sod, aerate, rake or till the soil to loosen compacted areas and churn up some breathing room for the roots. As with seed, after laying down sod, you must water it consistently. Sod usually roots two weeks after installation.

A few down sides to sod are the cost, limited choice, and hard labor involved in laying it. Because sod is mature turf that was torn up from the soil and rolled or cut into portable squares to serve as readymade grass in a different location, the hard work is mostly done. Sod is heavy and usually requires a truck or special vehicle to haul enough to fill a front lawn. This is why sodding is generally left to the pros. Sod is also limited in variety—you get what is available. And you'll pay for it ten-fold, compared to seed.

PREPARE SOIL FOR SOD just as you would for seed. Sod also requires good soil contact and constant watering for the first two weeks so roots establish.

Spot Treatment

Perhaps your seeding project is on a smaller scale—not the whole front yard, just that nasty brown spot that seems to grow larger by the week. Disease and weeds can prey on even the highest-quality turf, and the area in which your dog takes care of business probably isn't green. You can patch these spots easily by using seed or a clever sod method by which you harvest your own from a discreet area.

Steps for Seeding a Spot

1. Remove the dead spot with a shovel, digging straight down into the ground. The hole should be about 12 inches (30.5 cm) deep. Remember, you want to remove the damaged-root zone and clear out the area, so you can start fresh.

2. Fill the hole with topsoil. Choose a loamy soil that will provide plenty of nutrients for new seeds to establish. Tamp down the soil so it is level with the turf.

3. Seed the area with a mix that matches your existing turfgrass. This is why knowing your grass type is important. If you seed with a variety that behaves much differently, the spot of new grass will look like an obvious patch job.

4. Topcoat, or topdress, the area by covering it with a layer of hay or a paper mulch product to protect it from losing moisture and from birds, who like to dine on seeds.

5. Water the spot, taking care to keep the area moist for the few first weeks, while seeds germinate and sprout.

Sod It Yourself

Say you don't know what type of turfgrass your lawn is, and you don't want to take the chance of choosing the wrong seed for a highly visible brown spot. You can patch it with turf from a secret spot in your lawn—an area in a far back corner, for example. Call it the nursery area. Dig out a section to fit the brown spot in your front yard. Follow the steps above, digging up the bad spot and filling it in with a loamy topsoil that will accept new roots. Place your homemade sod on the spot and water it in thoroughly.

This patchwork process works well if you have creeping turfgrass. But because tall fescues and other bunch grasses cannot spread laterally, when you dig up a spot in the back, it will not fill in with new growth unless you seed it. Know your turfgrass type, so you can modify your care practices and repair strategies.

CHAPTER 2

Healthy Soil

Nutrient-rich soil is a satisfying four-course meal for turf, complete with air, water, organic matter, and mineral particles. When soil is deprived, turfgrass goes hungry. In rich, balanced soil, turfgrass will thrive and stave off weeds, insects, and disease.

We often don't realize that the culprit of our lackluster lawn is what lies beneath it. We assume that our turf is thirsty and needs more water. Maybe fertilizer will green up the brown areas. We blame the weather, or we call in landscapers to evaluate the property. We chose the right plant for the right place, so why won't it grow? We look around our properties for clues, but often, the root of the problem is underground.

Soil is the last place we look when our turf isn't performing as expected. The saying "Manage the roots, sell the shoots" describes the importance of soil management in the turfgrass industry.

Healthy soil is like a sturdy foundation for a home. You can build an elaborate structure—the envy of the neighborhood—but if you don't bother to construct a sturdy frame, the beauty will crumble fast. Similarly, what's the point of spending time caring for your lawn, and investing in products and equipment to give it the very best manicure, if you ignore the soil?

You can compare turfgrass's dependency on healthy soil to the way in which tomato plants fare in loamy, rich topsoil. You probably prepare your garden or a container with topsoil before dropping young tomato plants into their new home. Knowing that you can't simply clear out

a spot in your mulch bed for your tomato plants, you till and amend the ground, so your fruit will grow red and ripe.

We sometimes forget that grass is a plant, too. Each blade retains water; every root relies on nutrients from soil. The catch is, our properties often do not provide the best accommodations for turfgrass establishment. New construction leaves the land pitted with upturned bedrock and leftover scraps. Stripping lots to build usually means eliminating layers of organic matter. And in mature lawns, our turfgrass can deplete the soil's nutrients over time—its roots can grow deep and tangle, fighting for minerals and water.

There are ways to improve both situations. The first is to understand your soil profile. What really lies beneath?

Soil Profile

Under every lush lawn is supportive soil that provides the proper balance of nutrients to feed turf the nitrogen, phosphorus, and potassium it requires. Ideal soil retains moisture, so roots have plenty to drink, and is porous enough to hold oxygen—also necessary for healthy root establishment. The best soil is well-structured loam with equal parts of sand, clay, and organic matter, so nutrients don't leach, or filter through soil without enriching it.

Of course, too much of a good thing can ruin your turf. Soil that holds too much water and doesn't drain will leave puddles on a lawn. And if soil contains too much oxygen but little organic matter, it won't retain water. Soil composed of too much clay compacts easily, and overly sandy soils will not retain water or nutrients; instead, they slide right through the porous structure.

The fact is, most of us aren't working with ideal soil—especially if our home is in a new subdivision, where construction practices can strip away up to 7 inches (17.8 cm) of topsoil to grade land and clear space for homes. That leaves subsoil as the top layer, and this dense ground is usually infertile.

Before you can improve or amend your soil, you need to evaluate it. Think of this process as conducting a background check on the soil—getting the dirt. You want to find out what's going on down there, so you can make wise decisions about how to care for your lawn.

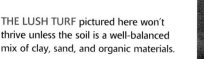

THE LUSH TURF pictured here won't thrive unless the soil is a well-balanced mix of clay, sand, and organic materials.

Physical Examination

First, let's discuss some physical attributes of soil, including texture and particle size. There are two types of soil: clay and sand. In a perfect lawn, your soil is a combination of each. A balance allows soil to retain water but not at the expense of proper drainage. The right sand-clay combination provides an appropriate mix of oxygen and organic matter, so that turfseed can establish and grow dense.

Not sure what your soil composition is? Simple observation will teach you quite a bit about your soil's habits. Do you notice puddles of water collecting on your lawn, or do you water every day and wonder why the turf feels crispy? Visually survey your property, and tune into its texture.

Clay Soils

Composed of very fine particles, clay soils compact easily but excel at retaining water and nutrients. Imagine a clump of clay doused with water. The material absorbs the moisture, becoming soupy, then thick and sticky, like cement. Clay molds to the touch and compacts easily.

WATER SHOULD PENETRATE the soil, so deep-growing roots can drink up moisture.

Soil that is too compacted will not absorb water or drain properly. When clay soil dries out, it tends to harden and crack. Roots have a tough time penetrating this type of surface.

Sandy Soils

Characterized by large, grainy particles, sandy soils permit water to flow freely from the surface—too freely, in fact. Trapping moisture and nutrients in sandy soil presents a challenge. The soil is never quite saturated. Imagine waves crashing on a beach. Moments after water recedes from the shore, sand drinks up any standing water and stiffens, like pavement, so you can walk across its surface. A sandy soil exhibits this same behavior—which explains why turfgrass planted in it dries out quickly. Roots get a quick drink of water as it passes through the soil, but they never have an opportunity to imbibe.

Fertility Factor

Healthy soil contains essential elements that help turf grow: nitrogen, phosphorus, and potassium. Besides these Big Three, which you'll find in all fertilizers, your soil should contain micronutrients from organic material. Basically, organic matter consists of microorganisms that live in the ground—plants and animals that decompose into an equivalent of dessert for your soil.

Soil pH

Soil can only provide a receptive environment for plant growth if the pH is correct. Soil pH refers to its chemistry: acidic or alkaline. The pH scale runs from 1 (very acidic) to 14 (very alkaline). When soil pH is below 7, it is acidic and you can face toxicity problems. On the other hand, an alkaline soil with a pH much higher than 7 is probably deficient in nutrients. The ideal soil pH is from 6 to 7.

You can do everything right for your lawn—choose the right seed, water properly, and apply the correct fertilizer products. But if your soil pH is 4, your turfgrass will not perform well. The good news? You can restore balance to your soil through specialty lawn-care products. But first, you must find out exactly what your soil status is.

AN ALKALINE SOIL PH could be a sign that you water too frequently. The quality of water you use to irrigate your yard will also affect your soil pH. If your soil is too acidic, reevaluate how much fertilizer you use. Are you applying it with a heavy hand? Most fertilizer consists of salts, and too much of it can offset the pH of your soil.

Take a Sample, Check the Status

Think of a soil test as an annual physical—important for uncovering information about your soil that you can't see. Results from a soil test will help you prescribe a lawn care program (see Chapter 4) that suits your property. For example, a soil pH that is too high may be deficient in iron and manganese. You can use ammonium sulfate fertilizer to lower the pH. Applications of general sulfur can lower the pH, as well. Knowing your soil pH will help treat your turf with the nutrients it needs.

You can purchase at-home test kits and check the pH level yourself, or you can send a soil sample to a reliable lab. University extension services generally offer soil testing for free, and you can be sure their results are accurate. Also, an extension service will help you understand what the test results really mean. Then, an agronomist or turfgrass specialist can make recommendations on various products or amendments to help balance the pH of your soil.

Whether you test soil yourself or rely on a lab, you'll need to collect the soil samples. If there is one key to remember when doing this, it's location, location, location. Results from a soil test are only as good as the sample you send in. So, take several core samples from random spots in your lawn to collect the best, representative example of what lies beneath.

The Steps

1. Collect Soil Cores: Using a shovel or small soil probe, randomly collect several core samples from the turfgrass area (as many as ten cores). Cores should be taken at a depth of 4 to 6 inches (10.2 to 15.2 cm) and measure about ¾ of an inch in diameter.

2. Mix Soil: Combine cores in a clean, plastic (not metal) bucket. Thoroughly mix the soil, and remove enough to fill the container provided by the soil laboratory or included in the at-home kit.

3. Info, Please: Fill out the information sheet from the lab, and send in the sample for evaluation. Most labs will return results in a few weeks.

4. Analyze This: If you are using an at-home test kit, follow the package directions for performing the analysis. The kits will measure levels of the Big Three (nitrogen, potassium, and phosphorus) and soil pH. An information packet will provide recommendations on amending the soil to improve its condition.

If you have trouble reading a soil test report, call a university extension service for help. Reports may look different, but they all contain the following information:

- Soil pH level
- Available nutrients and micronutrients
- Soluble salts and sodium (lower is better)
- Organic matter
- The soil's capacity for holding nutrients (higher is better)
- A recommendation for amending the soil

Solving Soil Issues

So, your soil isn't perfect—it's a bit acidic, it lacks organic materials, and the clay structure is compacted after years of heavy traffic. Relax. This is a portrait of most suburban lawns, which probably were established on soil stripped of nutrients during construction. Also know that most soils tend to be acidic. If you don't aerate annually and your soil is clay, you will inevitably face compaction issues.

These are all problems you can fix.

Low pH

If test results indicate low pH, the soil is probably deficient in calcium, magnesium, and potassium. A material that contains some form of lime will help raise soil pH. Limestone products are available in various particle sizes: pulverized, granular, pelletized, and hydrated. The finer the limestone's particles, the more rapidly it will work. Different soils require varying amounts of lime to level the pH. For example, clay soils require more lime because of their less porous texture. Hydrated lime can burn grass when applied at high rates, so most homeowners choose ground products that are easily applied with a spreader. For best results, apply lime two to three months before planting to allow time for it to neutralize acidic soils.

High pH

Alkaline soils with high pH levels are not as common as acidic soils, and restoring their deficiencies in iron requires elemental sulfur. *Note:* If your pH is high in calcium carbonate, sulfur will not lower the pH level. You can purchase fertilizers that contain sulfate to help balance pH levels. Look for a nitrogen (N), phosphorus (P), potassium (K) rating of 21-3-21. The most dramatic way to change soil pH is to apply sulfur fertilizer forms that contain ammonium. Sulfate will work, but it is slower acting.

Compacted Soil

The best way to loosen up soil to make room for root growth is to aerate it, a process that literally airs out the soil. This is performed by a vertical mower with tines that pull up plugs of soil. You can rent a core aerator machine, or you call a landscape contractor and order the service, which is usually scheduled in the fall. We'll walk you through the steps of aerating your own lawn in the Weekend Workshops section of this book, on page 104.

Adding Amendments

The best time to manage structural issues is at the time of planting, when the soil is exposed and you can easily till in organic matter and other amendments. Structure refers to the soil's ratio of clay, sand, and organic matter. Amendment is a general term referring to organic matter or man-made materials mixed into the soil. Amending the soil improves its physical qualities or changes its composition, so it is more accommodating to plant growth. Once turf is mature, your ability to change its structure is limited.

The two main types of amendments are organic and inorganic materials.

Organic amendments are decomposed plants or organisms, including the following:

- **Peat moss**
- **Wood chips**
- **Grass clippings**
- **Straw**
- **Compost**
- **Manure**
- **Biosolids, a sewage byproduct**
- **Sawdust**
- **Wood ash**

Inorganic amendments are mined or man made and include the following:

- **Sand**
- **Pea gravel**
- **Perlite**
- **Tire chunks**
- **Vermiculite**

AFTER SPREADING amendments, pass over the area with a rototiller, to work the material into the soil.

RAKE UP LEFTOVER DEBRIS, such as stones that get turned up during the tilling process.

If your lawn is established, it's not too late to improve the soil through topdressing, which is accomplished by spreading humus or a thin layer of material over a lawn after aeration. The humus will gradually decompose and enrich soil beneath the turf stand.

Do not confuse amendments with mulch. Both are beneficial, but mulch is not designed to change soil structure. It sits on the soil surface, reducing evaporation and runoff, staving off weeds, and helping to moderate soil temperature. Mulch is also applied f or curb appeal. It dresses up beds and adds interest to a landscape.

Before you dig into an amendment or lawn renovation (topdressing) project, be sure to choose materials that will correct your soil structure. Based on the characteristics discussed earlier, you should know whether your soil is composed mostly of sand or clay. This will make a significant difference in the material you apply.

Improving Clay Soils

If you amend clay with sand, you'll get muck. Clay will fill in the porous areas of sand and form a sort of concrete wall, making it impossible for water to reach roots. What you'll end up with is water runoff and dead grass. Not good. Instead, choose peat moss or compost, which work well in heavy, clay soils, because they will increase porosity.

Improving Sandy Soils

Generally, the goal when amending sandy soils is to improve water retention and the ability to store nutrients. Milled peat moss works well to achieve this. You can purchase this type of material in bulk from big-box retailers and garden centers, some of which offer delivery service.

Soil amendments improve soil structure, providing a strong foundation for your lawn. The best amendments will achieve the following:

- Improve aeration
- Help soil retain water and nutrients
- Encourage drainage
- Promote root growth

A Word on Compost

Compost is an effective amendment for sand and clay, although if you compost material yourself, you should send a sample to a lab to test its salt content. Composted plant materials and sphagnum peat are low-salt options, but testing is always a good idea if the package does not indicate salt content. High salt concentrations plug up soil and reduce soil productivity for plant growth.

Water Works

Water is the elixir for growth, an essential during every stage of a turf plant's lifecycle—a constant. Water feeds seedlings, so they germinate into strong plants, and provides relief to an overheated lawn. When and how much you water your grass will determine its vitality. It's amazing that such a simple process requires a lot of care. Fortunately, there are technology and systems available to help lift the burden.

Water is one of the basic elements that sustains life. Without it, we get parched, then dehydrated. Eventually, our energy drains and we display signs of dehydration: dry skin, dry eyes, dry mouth, dry everything. Our bodies are more than 70 percent water. We need it—and so does turf.

We can down a glass of fluid to rehydrate, but watering our lawns requires more careful attention. The process is not as easy as connecting a hose to a sprinkler and turning on a water source. As with other turf care practices, watering also requires a knowledge of your soil and turf type and an awareness of obstacles imposed by the environment. What seems like the easiest of lawn care chores is the one that homeowners tend to neglect.

Perhaps the reason so many of us deprive our lawns of water, or soak it with too much, is that watering is easy, to a fault. We tend to switch on our sprinklers and forget about them for a few hours—the old "set and forget." Meanwhile, our lawns are subjected to the equivalent of a flood. Water runs off the surface and never makes it to thirsty roots. Or, we go on vacation and allow our turf to wilt and dry out; when we return, we make up for lost time by overwatering, expecting the grass to green up, as though H_2O were a magic potion. Neither of these watering techniques benefit your lawn.

Water wisdom starts with a basic knowledge of how turf plants process water. But proper watering practices in any climate are based on two keys: soil and weather. These variables will dictate the amount of water your property needs and how frequently you should water.

Thirsty Turf

Turfgrass does not absorb moisture from the top of the plant—blades don't have mouths that drink up fluids. Rather, the roots are responsible for taking in water. Water percolates through the soil and seeps down several inches to the root zone. There, roots act as giant straws, sucking in moisture. If water doesn't soak into the soil and reach those roots, your grass may look wet on the surface, but it won't actually reap the benefits of watering.

You will notice when turf is thirsty because it will wilt or change colors. Do you see footprints on your lawn? When grass loses its bounce, it is giving in to drought stress—wilting. If your once-green grass turns bluish, lack of water is probably the cause. Without water, turfgrass loses the energy to green-up, grow, and thrive.

Turf plants constantly need water. They need water the way people need air. In fact, the way plants process water is similar to how humans breathe. Plants undergo transpiration and respiration. Transpiration is the passage of water through a plant from the roots to the vascular system and into the atmosphere. Respiration is oxygen transfer. Plants return to the environment what we consume, which is why they are an irreplaceable component of our ecosystem.

THIS LARGE EXPANSE OF TURF is exposed to full sun most of the day. A regular watering schedule will prevent the slightly sloped property from drying out during the midday heat.

Transpiration is the passage of water through a plant from the roots through the vascular system and into the atmosphere.

How Often, How Much?

So we know that plants need water. How much they need depends on the rainfall and soil content in your area, as well as turfgrass variety. Some species are designed to withstand drought; others require consistent watering to thrive. Water requirements for various turf plants depend on root depth and drought tolerance. For example, the deeper the roots, the longer grass can go without watering, because it taps into moisture stores deep beneath the surface. Shallow roots tend to grow in soils that do not permit water to sink deep down into the ground.

Roots and Soil

In the perfect lawn, loamy soil and deep-rooted turfgrass provide easy access for water. It would seep into the soil, reach well-established roots, and never run off the soil surface or collect in messy puddles. But slopes, compacted soil, and shallow roots are obstacles in many lawns. The key to a successful lawn is to work around tricky subsurface conditions that can prevent water uptake.

We discussed in Chapter 2 why soil is the foundation for healthy turf. Soil is a filter through which water must pass. Depending on the soil density, the earth will allow only a certain amount of water to enter its territory.

Water does not easily penetrate heavy clay soils. If you water too long, the moisture that the soil doesn't accept runs off the turf surface, forming puddles in low-lying areas—a muddy situation. Even worse, when water doesn't penetrate the soil, roots will not grow deep. Why would they go where there is no water? When water never sinks more than 2 inches (5 cm) into the soil, roots grow near the soil surface, to drink up the moisture.

Shallow roots result in a weak turf plant. Shallow-rooted turf also needs to be watered more often, because the unabsorbed water evaporates quickly.

The bonus with clay soils is that their rate of evaporation is much slower than that of sandy soils. In general, turf specialists advocate deep watering for deep root growth, but, in clay soils, that water sometimes won't have an opportunity to seep down if you overflow the lawn with water all at once. By watering more frequently for shorter periods of time, water will eventually work its way deeper into clay soils, promoting deep root growth. Think of this as feeding your lawn mini meals, rather than a seven-course dinner all at once. Smaller doses of water on a frequent basis will ensure that the soil area where roots reside stays wet.

Sandy soils are a different animal. Because sand doesn't trap moisture, water slips right through a grainy profile. Although it soaks in easily, it evaporates quickly, so roots don't always get the nice drink they need. Keeping in mind the agronomist's rule of thumb—deep watering promotes deep root growth—the best method for watering turf with a sandy soil profile is to water regularly, and let the water sink in deep. Unfortunately, watering for longer periods of time doesn't guarantee that sandy soil will retain moisture. So, if you plan to reseed your lawn, this is the ideal time to improve water absorbency by adding amendments to stabilize sandy soil. (See Chapter 2, page 33.)

GO DEEP

HOW DEEPLY SHOULD YOU WATER? Think about how Mother Nature waters your lawn during a steady, hard rain. Turf agronomists recommend a minimum of 4 to 6 inches (10.2 to 15.2 cm) in normal conditions.

Aeration will speed up percolation rate if you have a problem with compacted soil. Especially with clay soils, aeration will literally air out the site and allow water to permeate thick turf and reach roots.

Timing Is Everything

Where watering is concerned, there are two types of homeowners. One waters every day, wakes up early to turn on the sprinkler, and never forgets to give the lawn a good soak on weekends. The other allows grass to evolve into a strawlike weed patch before unwinding the tangled hose, which probably hasn't been touched all season. By then, it's too late. Watering dead grass is a waste of time and water. It's not going to perk up into the green yard you had before you left for a three-week vacation—during the hottest month of the year, of course.

Ideally, you should monitor your lawn on a regular basis for wilting and color changes. Weigh in weather conditions, and know exactly what type of soil lies beneath that beautiful bed of turf before you hook up the sprinkler. Remember, weather and soil determine when and how much to water.

Here are a couple of watering practices to keep in mind.

First, most turf needs about 1 inch (2.5 cm) of water per week. *Most* is the operative word. If your turfgrass is a drought-tolerant variety, it will thrive on much less, and if you experience a solid week of rain, the excess moisture won't hurt your turf. The most it will do is create a few temporary puddles and muddy spots, which will eventually dry out.

That said, you can only fill the pores of your soil so much. If you water excessively, the result is runoff. So watch your lawn for clues (puddles, for example).

Second, it's important to time your watering properly. Ideally, you should water your lawn before dawn or after dark. Midday is the least efficient time to water, for a couple of reasons. Water you apply in mid-afternoon will not be absorbed as deeply by the soil, because the sun will capture it first. Sunlight causes water to evaporate faster, so roots work to take up moisture at a higher rate. You'll waste water and force roots to work harder, potentially stressing out turf plants. Also, daytime watering adds one more stress to city water systems, which work overtime when residents wake up and take showers.

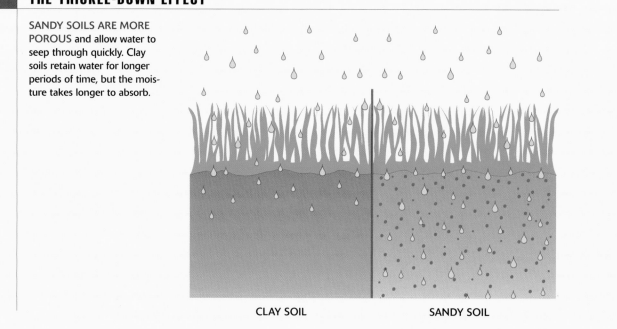

THE TRICKLE-DOWN EFFECT

SANDY SOILS ARE MORE POROUS and allow water to seep through quickly. Clay soils retain water for longer periods of time, but the moisture takes longer to absorb.

CLAY SOIL   SANDY SOIL

How Often Should You Water?

Establish a regular watering schedule to ensure your lawn gets consistent, adequate moisture. Assuming that the weather isn't excessively hot or unusually rainy, and that your turf is healthy, the average watering frequency is every other day or every third day, in normal conditions. The catch is, what is normal in your region and appropriate for your turf truly dictates the amount of water your turf needs to thrive.

The best way to address the "how often" question is to act as the official meteorologist for your property. Are you expecting heavy rains in the afternoon? Well then, soaking your lawn that morning is probably unnecessary. Has a drought already driven your lawn into dormancy? Then leave it be. Better to wait on watering than shock turf into a cycle of complete dehydration followed by a water binge. Allowing turf to die out before you water it is like waiting too long to eat a meal—you sabotage your body's metabolism and cannot efficiently process nutrients. Your turf experiences the same stress when you deprive it of water for long periods of time, then desperately switch on sprinklers, hoping to restore its green color. By that point, turf plants are too worn out to respond.

WET OR DRY?

A NOTE ON WATERING IN DRY WEATHER: Decide whether you will allow grass to go dormant or to water it regularly to keep it green. Either choice is fine—just decide and commit.

If you want grass to retain its luster during a dry spell, water deeply in early morning or late evening (in most regions).

THE PRO: Your grass will not go dormant.

THE CON: Your water bill will increase, and you must remember to water daily.

THE OBSTACLE: Some areas impose water restrictions during times of drought. If you live in one of these areas, watering daily might not be an option.

If you decide to allow grass to go dormant, in most circumstances, it will slowly regain color and wake up once the dry spell ends.

THE PRO: You will save on water bills and allow nature to take its course.

THE CON: Your lawn will turn brown, and there is a chance that your turf will burn out completely.

THE OBSTACLE: Avoid the temptation to water if turf is already turning brown—by then, the damage is done. You lessen the chance of it regenerating by teasing it with sporadic drinks of water.

Ways to Water

SELECT FROM VARIOUS STYLES of hose-end sprinklers, taking care to choose the style based on the shape of your property.

You can use several systems to deliver water to your lawn, including various types of hose-end sprinklers and irrigation systems, which are generally installed by professionals. The choice is yours. Before making it, consider your watering mindset. If watering is a hassle, and you're likely to forget to switch on sprinklers early in the morning, then an irrigation system is a reliable solution. On the other hand, if your climate delivers plenty of rain, and you rarely have to water manually, a hose-end sprinkler is an affordable and logical choice.

The Hook Up: Sprinklers

Watering by hand requires time, to set up sprinklers, and attention, to ensure you don't "set and forget" them. Hose-end sprinklers provide the deep watering turf needs, but beware of the tendency to overwater when using pulsating or oscillating (rainbow) sprinklers. If you leave sprinklers on for hours while you go about your day, the result is a high water bill and a sopping lawn.

Another warning with hose-end sprinklers: observe water distribution for uniformity. Think about the shape of your lawn (excluding flower beds). Is it square? Do beds create a circle of turf? Base your choice of sprinkler on the shape of your lawn. Oscillating sprinklers work well in square turf areas, while pulsating sprinklers that spit out water at a radius will deliver water uniformly in circle-shaped lawns.

Oscillating Sprinklers

Oscillating sprinklers, also called flip-flop sprinklers, deliver a moving rainbow of water. Droplets fall in a neat, rectangular pattern. Oscillating sprinklers work well in side yards, long stretches of turf, or square lawns, if the sprinkler is positioned to fully cover the area.

PERFECT TIMING

RETAIL OUTLETS carry hose-end timers, which allow you to program sprinklers to turn on and off each day. These can run on batteries and are easy to set.

THIS MULTIDIRECTIONAL SPRINKLER (ABOVE) disperses water from the top and all sides of the head attachment. Soaker hoses and drip irrigation systems, such as the one shown at the right, are ideal for watering plant beds.

Pulsating Sprinklers

Also called impact or rotary sprinklers, pulsating sprinklers shoot out water in a circular pattern and can be adjusted to cover a slice of your lawn or a fairly large area.

Soaker Hoses

Soaker hoses are part of the drip-irrigation family, and you can find them in garden stores. The hose, which looks like a tube with tiny holes in it, attaches to a spigot. Small streams of water spray from the tubing. Place soaker hoses in flower beds or along narrow turf pathways—areas in which oscillating and pulsating sprinklers would be overbearing. (Learn how to install a drip irrigation system on page 124.)

Irrigation Systems

In-ground irrigation systems are an efficient, convenient means of delivering even water coverage to your property, for many reasons. You can time them to water in the middle of the night or early morning, long before your alarm sounds. You can program them to water your lawn while you are vacation. They do not forget to water—and we're all guilty of this, sometimes.

Generally speaking, the watering efficiency achieved through in-ground irrigation will offset the price of the system, installation, and annual upkeep. Because irrigation systems water your lawn consistently, you actually save water because you'll avoid the feast-and-famine approach to watering turf. (Those feasts when you make up for lost watering time can hike up your water bill and stress out overworked turf plants.

A professional can install your in-ground irrigation system. You can do the job yourself, but an irrigation technician will know what system design and components best fits your needs. He or she will divide your lawn into designated watering zones—necessary, because water service lines cannot provide enough water to irrigate an entire yard at once. Zones, also called water stations, allow the irrigation system to water one area of the turf at a time without taxing the city water supply.

THE POP-UP SPRAY HEADS in this irrigation system (above) rise from the ground and water the property on a regular schedule. A controller programmed with watering times alerts the system to turn on and off.

Irrigation systems include the following components:

Controller: This device turns the system on and off, according to preset times.

Sprinkler Heads: Available in spray heads or rotary heads and pop-up or fixed styles. Spray heads are generally placed no more than 15 feet (4.5 m) apart. They pop up during watering and retract below the turf line to allow for easy mowing. Rotary heads are used in open spaces and disperse water 30 feet (9 m) or more.

Sprinkler Nozzle: The cap of the sprinkler head through which water passes as it is dispersed. You can choose nozzles that distribute more or less water per minute, depending on your watering needs.

Valves: Control water in various zones.

Sensors: Interrupt the electrical flow from the controller to the valve. Rain sensors prevent the system from watering the lawn if it is already wet. Freeze sensors control valves when the temperature is below freezing, so the system will shut off when the temperature drops. Sensors do not interfere with the controller's program, so if you set the system to turn on at 6 AM and the rain sensor shuts off your valves on Tuesday because of precipitation, the system will maintain its program and turn on at 6 AM Wednesday, as scheduled.

Rotary Head

NOTICE THE NOZZLE on top of this fixed spray head.

THIS LANDSCAPE BED might represent one zone, or water station.

Even Coverage

Whether you choose to install an irrigation system or rely on hose-end sprinklers to water your lawn, even coverage is important. Otherwise, you'll wind up with a lawn that has a split personality—portions of it missed by the water stream will look thirsty, and areas that collect too much water can form muddy spots and potentially suffer from root rot.

Here's a trick to help determine whether your water delivery system is playing fair: Think of your lawn as a checkerboard with 5-foot (1.5-meter) squares. To determine whether your sprinkler is thoroughly covering all areas of your lawn, place a clear plastic cup in each square. The cups will form a grid pattern. Turn on your sprinklers or irrigation system for a half hour. After this time, measure the water in each cup. If you notice that some cups lack water, adjust the irrigation heads so they distribute more water in that area. For hose-end sprinklers, ensure that you adjust or rotate the sprinkler to the area of your lawn that is deprived of water. This primitive test will offer a clear picture of water coverage.

Tricky Situations

Because weather is unpredictable and lawns vary in shape, size, and geography, watering practices must take into account your microclimate. If your backyard slopes into a creek and you live in a windy region, you can count on these two variables botching your watering plan some days.

Here are some ways to get around tricky situations.

Slopes: Take care when watering sloped surfaces. Water will roll down the surface and collect at the bottom, forming a puddle and damaging turf. Meanwhile, turf at the top of the hill will dry out. The best way to manage slopes is to water lightly and frequently. Allow water to soak in but not to run off. There are no exact time recommendations for watering slopes, so you'll have to spend time observing how your turf responds to watering. Adjust times as needed.

Wind: When the wind kicks up, the water your sprinkler shoots to one side of the lawn can drift to the other, delivering a double-dose of moisture to part of your property. If possible, avoid watering in exceptionally windy conditions. If you must water when it's windy, move your sprinkler head frequently to compensate for displaced water.

Seeding: Remember the water-deeply-and-less-often rule? Forget this when establishing a new lawn. Seed needs a daily dose of water to germinate, so keep the ground moist. Watering frequently for short periods of time is the best way to do this.

Water Conservation

The type of turfgrass suitable for lawns wasn't meant to thrive in every climate. If you take a plane ride across southwestern states and notice a patch of emerald green in a desert area, you probably wonder what's wrong. The green island surrounded by sand and rock looks unnatural. Don't force green into your landscape if nature didn't intend it to be that way.

If you live in a drought climate, consider alternatives like xeriscaping, a landscaping method that uses plants that require little to no water once established.

Regardless of where you live—in a desert climate or on a subtropical coastline—you should take measures to conserve water. Here are some ideas to get you started:

- **Mow your lawn** at a higher than normal height
- **Avoid applying fertilizer** that promotes growth and will further stress the turf
- **Control thatch and soil compaction** so the water you do use is used efficiently
- **Do not allow** the water to run off onto sidewalks or driveways

THE SLOPE IN THIS PROPERTY requires careful attention when watering.

CHAPTER 4

Get the Best Green

Roll out the lush green carpet to guests—create an emerald entryway to your home. Curb appeal is just a few steps away. Products designed to enhance the color, vigor, and overall turfgrass health are within reach. Pair them with the best basic lawn care practices, and you will quench your lawn's appetite for a balanced meal, while satisfying your own desire for a dream lawn. Consider this your lawn care crash course, a down-and-dirty guide for how and when to fertilize and apply herbicides and what tools you need to get the job done.

Imagine a healthy, resilient lawn, one that looks painstakingly cared for, so green and manicured, it could be a golf course. Surely, a secret formula—a fertilizer or miracle product—is responsible for that picture-perfect turf. Green that good can't be natural, can it?

This assumption isn't too far off base. Because we often encourage turf to grow in challenging conditions, it needs extra nutrients to achieve the color, density, and longevity we expect. A proper lawn care program is the key to promoting turf growth and managing weeds, insects, and disease. It includes fertilizer, herbicides, and, when needed, products to prevent or control insects and pests.

Where you live and the type of grass you grow will determine the kind of lawn care program you use. Turfgrass variety also affects lawn behavior when you apply fertilizers and herbicides. We'll discuss appropriate fertilization and weed-control programs for cool- and warm-season grasses and ways to maximize the performance of your lawn year-round.

A PERFECT GREEN isn't always what nature intended for certain turfgrass species. When properly cared for, however the most common varieties, such as Kentucky Bluegrass, produce dense, rich, green leaves.

Variations on Green

Before we delve into how fertilizer works and when it is best applied, let's erase the myth that only green grass is healthy grass. That's just not the case.

We mistakenly associate turf performance with its color, assuming that a lawn that isn't a perfect green must be undernourished. While turfgrass certainly lets us know that it needs water, nutrients, and T.L.C. by turning brown, color alone isn't an indication that it needs fertilizer. After all, turfgrass varieties come in a spectrum of colors, ranging from blue-gray to yellow-green and lime. So, before assuming that your lawn is doomed to die out, be sure you understand the physical qualities your turfgrass *should* display when healthy.

Imagine the outcome if a homeowner with warm-season grass, which goes dormant in winter, panics when his lawn starts turning brown in the fall. Determined to reverse the situation, he applies a heavy dose of fertilizer, hoping it will green up. The problem: warm-season grasses need nutrients the most during their growing season, which is spring. This homeowner is wasting money and product, and his lawn probably won't cooperate.

The lesson: before fertilizing or applying any product, know your turf type and understand its response to air temperature (the season) and moisture.

Fertilizer and the Big Three

Fertilizer is credited for sprucing up a lawn's color and helping it grow. Homeowners generally turn to fertilizer first when grass loses its luster or turns brown after suffering a drought. With an array of fertilizers available in retail stores, finding a fix to restore a lawn seems as easy as buying a bag of product.

Of course, fertilization isn't that simple—but it isn't rocket science, either. If you understand the chemistry behind the three major components of fertilizer, you can choose and apply the correct product for your lawn. The Big Three are nitrogen, phosphorus, and potassium (N, P, and K), and you will find the ratio of these three elements listed in that order on every package. For example, if a label reads 1-2-1, it contains one part nitrogen, two parts phosphorus, and one part potassium. Depending on the ratio of these three elements,

a fertilizer formula can help turf look greener, grow faster, or wear longer.

The best fertilization program feeds turf with a balance of these three nutrients throughout the growing season. Different N-P-K ratings are appropriate for different situations: in spring, after seeding a lawn, and before winter dormancy (for cool-season grasses). Following is how N, P, and K fortify turfgrass.

Nitrogen: The First Responder

Nitrogen is responsible for color. Think of it as the show-me element that provides the visual results you expect when you apply product to your lawn. Nitrogen gives you instant gratification in the form of green-up. It helps the plant metabolize and produce leaf growth. More is not necessarily better, however; if you apply too much nitrogen, grass will grow too fast. This doesn't necessarily hurt the lawn—it just means you'll mow it more often than you want to.

You can purchase fertilizer with slow- or quick-release nitrogen. You also can find formulations that combine both types. Turfgrass reacts similarly to both kinds of nitrogen (color and leaf growth); the difference between them is response time. Quick-release nitrogen is water-soluble and dissolves quickly. Grass greens up more quickly than with slow-release formulas, which release nitrogen over time. However, quick-release nitrogen does not last as long as slow-release formulas. When applied heavily to a lawn, rain or heavy irriga-

NITROGEN (A), PHOSPHORUS (B), AND POTASSIUM (C) provide a balanced meal for turf.

Any fertilizer spill, whether liquid or granular, should be cleaned up immediately. Do not leave open bags or containers where they might topple over. Also avoid spills by not overfilling spreaders or spray tanks. If you spill granular product on a hard surface, sweep it up right away and use it as instructed. If you spill a liquid product, prevent the product from entering storm drains. You can purchase absorbent materials to help you contain liquid spills.

tion can cause quick-release nitrogen to run off and wash into the nearest drainage gutter, presenting a clear environmental hazard and leaving your turf without its nutrient benefits. On the other hand, if not enough moisture exists to dissolve the nitrogen, it will sit on the grass plant and burn its leaves. Correct application rates are key. (See Calibration 101 on page 60.)

Slow-release nitrogen helps turf maintain color and recover from drought or dormancy. If you apply fertilizer with slow-release nitrogen in the spring, and an early-summer drought drains color from your lawn, slow-acting nitrogen is still working its magic. A fall application of fertilizer with slow-release nitrogen will help cool-season grasses maintain better color during the winter months. Slow-release nitrogen is in it for the long haul.

The best choice is a product that contains both slow- and quick-release nitrogen. A balance of these elements gives your lawn the best of both types: fast green-up from the quick-release nitrogen and long-lasting results from slow-release nitrogen, which continue to provide nutrients over eight to ten weeks, or more.

Phosphorus: Feeding the Seed

Phosphorus, the second number in the N-P-K sequence, promotes root growth, which is especially important for seedlings. If you are establishing cool-season grasses, such as Kentucky bluegrass, a fertilizer with a greater ratio of phosphorus to nitrogen and potassium helps the plants' root system mature more quickly. The same ratio applies to overseeding warm-season grasses with varieties such as annual ryegrass. Overseeding is practiced in southern and southwest climates, where warm-season

lawns go dormant and turn strawlike and brown during winter. By overseeding a warm-season lawn with annual ryegrass, the newly planted seed will grow quickly over the dormant turf and stay green throughout the winter, while the primary warm-season turf is brown. When the dormant warm-season grass takes over again in spring, the annual ryegrass dies out.

Unlike nitrogen, phosphorus requires more time to act. You may not necessarily see results, as it promotes growth of the turf plant underneath the soil surface. However, after a few weeks, seedlings should be well rooted, and the nitrogen will begin to work its magic, by encouraging the roots to produce healthy leaves.

When feeding a newly established lawn, choose fertilizers with ratios such as 1-2-1. This is a common formulation you can find in most brands at mass retailers.

Potassium: In for the Long Haul

Think of potassium (K) as Old Reliable. Potassium protects turf during droughts and prevents winterkill in certain cool-season grasses, such as perennial ryegrass. Stronger doses of potassium are best in fall, when turf needs to build up stress resistance to survive temperature and moisture changes. With the help of potassium, grass stands a better chance of emerging in good health come spring.

Like phosphorus, potassium is slow acting, so the response time isn't immediate, but results are longer lasting. You can count on potassium to feed your lawn for months after your last fall application. When choosing a fall fertilizer for cool-season grasses, opt for an N-P-K ratio that is heavier in nitrogen and potassium. Turf will store nitrogen and utilize it throughout the winter, and potassium will help increase plant hardiness.

Fertilizer Application

The adage 'Timing is everything' is a fitting motto for any lawn care application, including fertilizer. Because our lawns wake up in the spring and go dormant in the fall, according to Mother Nature's clock, environmental clues signal the most suitable time to fertilize. This varies from region to region, however, and does not come with an alarm to warn us that our turf is ready for its first application of the year.

There are a few rules of thumb regarding fertilizer application. First, you must apply it more than once each year. We don't expect a multivitamin to contain enough nutrients to fuel our bodies for months. Our lawns need more than one dose of N-P-K, too. A single spring fertilization will not offer year-round guaranteed growth and turf health. For optimum performance, plan on fertilizing your property at least three times a year and, at lighter application rates, as often as five times a year. Think of this as feeding your turf a regular, balanced meal, to keep it strong and fend off weeds, insects, and disease.

Labels Tell All

Before purchasing or applying any lawn care product, check the label. Read it, understand it, trust it. Labels will indicate the ratio of N-P-K, and they will explain how much product to apply per square foot (m^2). They list all the active ingredients and explain proper usage for the product. Read all of this carefully.

Labels also provide critical safety information, such as the necessity for eye protection and gloves with handling. Remember that lawn care products are chemicals. Although they are safe and beneficial for turf, they can be harmful and dangerous to you, if they're accidentally ingested, spilled, or rubbed into the eyes. Treat the label as law, and wear recommended safety gear. (Sunglasses are an acceptable alternative for light-duty eye protection.)

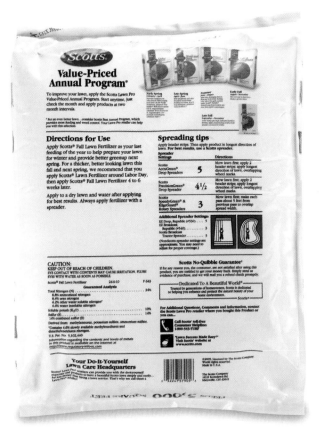

Fertilization Recommendations

Application timing varies according to your location and your turf type. Your lawn needs the most nutrients when it is active, during the growing season. This time frame varies for warm- and cool-season grasses.

Should you decide to forego the advice to fertilize several times a year and resort to a single application, do it in the fall for cool-season grasses and in the spring for warm-season grasses. Cool-season grasses that grow in the Midwest and Northeast need nutrients to last through the winter; a fertilizer application in the fall improves the odds of healthy spring green-up. Conversely, warm-season grasses that experience the most stress during summer need fertilizer in spring. This gives warm-season lawns staying power.

More is not better when it comes to applying fertilizer. In spring, excessive fertilization won't necessarily hurt the turf—you'll just have to cut it more often. But if you continue to apply fertilizer with a heavy hand during the summer, the following signs will indicate that your lawn is getting too much of a good thing:

- Plant leaves look succulent, and blades appear full of moisture
- Rubbing a blade between your fingers stains hands green
- Leaves flop over and look heavy or less vigorous
- Dense, green tufts grow in some areas that responded more readily to excessive nitrogen

WHEN TO FERTILIZE WHERE

Cool-Season Grasses

- **Spring:** Stimulation is your goal in the spring. Your fertilizer should promote growth without supplying turf with too much nitrogen.

- **Summer:** Summer is a better time for defense than offense. Take care not to fertilize too much during summer, when plants are under stress. Administer a couple of light fertilizer applications during summer months, but focus mostly on maintenance, such as controlling disease and insect problems.

- **Fall:** This is the most important time to fertilize your lawn, so that it will endure the winter. A fall fertilizer application feeds grass nutrients to store during dormancy.

Warm-Season Grasses

- **Spring:** This is the most important application time for grasses that grow during the warm season. They need nutrients to establish strong roots and promote leaf growth. Try a slow-release fertilizer in spring to prevent overly rapid growth.

- **Summer:** Maintenance during this steady growing season is critical. Apply frequent, light doses of fertilizer all summer.

- **Fall:** Warm-season grasses do not grow in the fall, so you can ease up on fertilization during this time of dormancy.

Leave product mixing to the pros. Always refer to the label for proper usage of all lawn care products and safe ways to apply them. Children and pets should not play on the property immediately following a lawn care application.

Your Customized Lawn Care Program

Fertilizer isn't all that turf needs to grow strong all year. If you don't control weeds, your fertilization efforts will feed unwanted grassy and broadleaf weeds, such as dandelions and crabgrass. Before long, your turf will compete with weeds, and guess which contender will eventually win?

What you need is a complete lawn care program to discourage unwanted weeds and pests and promote yearlong healthy turf growth.

In addition to fertilization, homeowners generally feel confident managing herbicide applications. In fact, many products are labeled "weed and feed" or are identified as preemergent/fertilizer blends. These formulas basically provide a two-for-one special that supplies turf with nutrients and weed control. These mixes are granular products. You'll also find liquid herbicides designed to spot-treat broadleaf and grassy weeds after they sprout. Lawn care professionals generally advocate liquids, because they provide more concentrated control and can be readily mixed with other formulas.

It's always a good idea to get advice from a professional. A licensed lawn care operator can best diagnose and recommend an individualized turf treatment program for insect and disease problems. They are more knowledgeable about disease pressures, proper timing for controlling insects such as grubs and fire ants, and preventive programs designed for properties with a history of disease and insect attacks. Essentially, a professional can write a prescription for your lawn. Because the products they use are commercial grade and generally not available off the shelf, you're paying for more concentrated, customized care.

However, you can easily manage lawn care applications with the array of products available at mass retailers. We'll explore some basic, easily manageable insecticide and pesticide treatments later on, but, for now, let's focus on herbicides—your best friend for weed removal.

Herbicides: Down with Weeds

Herbicides are weed control products and are available in several forms: selective, nonselective, contact, and systemic. *Selective* herbicides knock down certain weed species without affecting the growth of other plants. Most herbicides are selective. *Nonselective* herbicides wipe out all green plants. If you want to renovate or reestablish turf, a nonselective herbicide will clear the area. These products are also useful for spot treatment and removing weeds from sidewalks or driveway cracks. *Contact* herbicides are spot treatments that only affect the area touched by the formula. These generally require repeat applications. *Systemic* herbicides are slow acting, delivering weed-control substances to the turfgrass plant through its vascular system.

Assuming that you are not planning to eradicate all signs of green in your lawn, and your main goal is to stave off weeds, you'll want to use selective herbicides in two separate doses. These are called *preemergence* and *postemergence* applications.

Preemergence Applications

Preemergence herbicides control weeds before they sprout, creating a barrier of protection. Preemergence herbicide-fertilizer combinations, also called weed-and-feed, prevent weed establishment and provide nutrients to encourage healthy grass growth.

Think *pre*-emergence and *pre*-growing season. Your goal is to prevent weeds from emerging. Apply this round of herbicides in early spring, when you notice the forsythia blooming and the turfgrass growing more vigorous and green. Weeds tend to respond more quickly to temperature changes, so you can be sure that if the grass is growing, so are the weeds.

LIQUID OR GRANULAR?

GRANULAR AND LIQUID PRODUCTS both have merits. Liquids are ideal for spot-treating weeds, and granular products are more cost effective for covering a lot of ground. They're also often easier to apply. Following are the pros and cons of each.

Granular Enters plants through the root system. Time-released granules provide long-term benefits. However, because soil must absorb granules, some herbicide may wash away before roots can absorb it. Products can be applied less frequently at higher doses than liquids.

Liquid Leaves absorb liquid products, transferring them to grass roots, where they are stored. Results are quick, but heavy rain or water can wash away the herbicide before leaves absorb it. Also, liquids don't last as long as granular products and must be applied more frequently in lighter doses.

Postemergence Applications

Preemergence products will not knock down weeds that have already sprouted. This is where postemergence applications come in handy. You can use a liquid product to spray problem areas, taking care to apply the product well before temperatures climb. As a general rule, avoid applying postemergence herbicides once temperatures exceed 80 degrees Fahrenheit (27°C). At this point, the product will cook plant leaves, and, as you spot-treat weeds, you risk killing the healthy turfgrass that borders your target zone. Applied at the right time, postemergence products will not harm healthy turfgrass if your aim is off.

Herbicide Application Timing

Refer to your grass type before applying preemergence or postemergence herbicides. Cool-season grasses need weed control in the spring, with an additional application in late summer during the window of time when the summer stress is over but grass is still growing before winter dormancy.

Warm-season grasses are just the opposite. Weeds germinate during the winter, so you should apply herbicides in the fall. Choose a broadleaf herbicide, and spot treat weeds throughout the winter, when they are easily noticed.

Tools of the Trade

Granular and liquid products require special equipment for application. You can choose among various styles of spreaders and sprayers, which all do the same job but accomplish it differently.

Broadcast Spreader

Also called a rotary spreader, a broadcast spreader is the most goof-proof tool for applying granular products. A spinning disk at the hopper base throws granules in a fan-shaped swath. This action distributes granules evenly across the area, making it ideal for covering large spaces efficiently.

Drop Spreader

If you notice streaks of green in a lawn, you can probably guess a drop spreader was used to apply fertilizer. As the name implies, drop spreaders work by dropping fertilizer directly from the hopper onto the turf, in an even, defined path. The challenge: precision is absolutely necessary. When using a drop spreader, be sure to overlap each pass.

Hand-held Crank Spreader

These older models are not much more advanced than throwing granules onto your property by hand. But if your space is compact, the hand-held tool may do the job—it requires virtually no storage space and can finish the job quickly. Because they hold only a few pounds of fertilizer, crank spreaders are impractical for large areas.

Following are some tips for using a drop spreader:

ALWAYS CHECK that the spreader's release door is closed before filling the hopper with product. Set the spreader over a paved surface so you can easily sweep up spills.

WHEN OPERATING a drop spreader, always overlap passes. Line up the center of the spreader to the center of your last wheel track.

THE BEST WAY TO APPLY granular fertilizer accurately is to divide the application in half. Apply the first half in one direction, then apply the second half in a path perpendicular to your first pass. So, if you wheel the spreader toward your home on the first pass, for example, work toward your neighbor's house on the second round. A double pass method will prevent striping patterns that can result when you miss a spot.

Read the label before disposing of unused lawn care treatments. It will provide strict instructions to avoid environmental hazard.

Sprayers

Most of the sprayers available from retailers are back-pack or hand-held styles. A canister holds the liquid product, which is pressurized and distributed through a spray nozzle. Sprayers come in various sizes. Initially, you may feel more comfortable with a smaller, hand-held sprayer. But for larger jobs, a backpack sprayer is more useful; it holds a generous amount of product and is appropriate for most home lawns.

Hose Attachments and Premixed Formulas

You can purchase liquid product in a container that snaps onto a garden hose. This is a convenient method for some homeowners, but you may find that you can better control an application when using granular product and a spreader.

Calibration 101

Calibration is the process of setting your spreader to distribute granules at the rate given by the usage instructions on the product label. A little math is required to properly calibrate your spreader and determine the application rate for your property.

First, measure your lawn, either by using a wheel measure or by simply stepping off the length and width to get an estimate. Once you figure out the area, determine how much of the product you need. If the bag label specifies that the product will cover 5,000 square feet (464.5 square meters), and your property is 15,000 square feet (1,393.5 square meters), you will need three bags.

Next, check the label to determine the recommended calibration setting. If it specifies calibration letters ("Set spreader on E"), but your equipment is marked with numbers, estimate the appropriate setting by counting a number for every letter in the alphabet. In other words, the letter E is fifth in the alphabet, so you should set your spreader on number five.

You are now set to spread. Word of warning: don't pour the whole bag of product into the spreader—a mistake many novices make. Pace yourself, remembering to half the dose and apply it in two passes, to achieve even coverage. Referring back to our example, this means you would apply 1½ bags of product to your property on the first pass and the remainder of the three bags on the second, perpendicular, pass.

Do not apply granular products immediately after mowing your property—you won't see the spreader wheel tracks in the turf. Wait until a couple of days after mowing, when the spreader wheels leave temporary tracks and you can see where you hit and where you missed. Another trick is to apply granular products after an early morning dew. Remember to be sure and spread the product to the wheel of your last pass.

Oops! Did I Do That?

Fertilizer product application requires attention to detail and a bit of practice. Learn from these common mistakes and avoid getting burned during the process.

Overkill

Don't expect products to work immediately after you apply them. Impatient homeowners apply and then reapply when they don't see immediate results. Rather than eradicating target weeds, the overapplication burns holes in their lawn, and their property eventually looks like Swiss cheese. This is not the type of spot-treatment result they desired.

Your best bet is to choose a selective herbicide that targets your weed problem. Most off-the-shelf products are labeled for either grassy or broadleaf weeds. So, if dandelions are your problem, choose the broadleaf formula. If you notice unappealing, unruly tufts of foreign turf invading your lawn, choose the product for grassy weeds.

Stuck in Thatch

Thatch in your lawn has the same effect as wrapping it in plastic wrap. Water, nutrients, and lawn care products cannot be absorbed by a tight-knit lawn. Thatch is sometimes a product of overfertilization. The more you fertilize, the more dense your lawn becomes, because the product's nitrogen, phosphorus, and potassium contents spur growth. Be sure to aerate your lawn, to make room for the new growth that fertilizer promotes.

Bagging Up Benefits

You can mow your lawn after applying fertilizer or other lawn care products, but do not remove the clippings. When you bag them, you lose the benefits of the application. Leave clippings on the property for the first postapplication cut.

Burned by Spills

Always fill spreaders on a sidewalk, driveway, or other hard surface—not on your lawn. If you spill some granules, you can simply sweep up the extras. Otherwise, your spill spots will evolve into brown spots. The only way to fix a burnt-out patch of lawn is to rake out the dead grass and water the spot to promote spreading growth from surrounding turf plants. If you don't see results in three to four weeks, you'll most likely need to reseed that spot.

PART TWO

Total Lawn Care

For many of us, the outdoors is an escape, a place we go to tune out the noise of our busy lives and to clear our minds. Outside, we break the confines of cubicles, schedules, commitments, and walls of any kind. Nature slows us down. Grass grows only so fast, flowers bloom when they're good and ready, leaves fall when it's time. The hours we spend outdoors ground us.

And so our lawns become a retreat—our very own patchwork piece of earth that we must nurture. Many of us take this job very seriously. We care for our lawns, knowing that the lush, green results are a tribute to our hard work. A perfect cut, tidy edges, and rich emerald color are pay offs for T.L.C., Total Lawn Care. We've already covered the groundwork. Now, let's master the techniques to maintain your outdoor living room.

CHAPTER 5

Choosing a Mower

It's a hallmark investment, a rite of passage for first-time homeowners and a tool that earns prime space in most garages and sheds. Mowers are synonymous with lawn care. Perhaps you are purchasing your first mower or upgrading to a model more suitable to your changing lifestyle. Regardless, buying the right mower style, size, and accessories will help experienced operators and novices alike achieve an enviable cut.

Most consumers mow at 3 mph (5 kph), whether walking or riding. If your lawn is ½ acre (2,023 m²), and you operate a mower with a 21-inch (53.3 cm) cutting deck at 3 mph (5 kph), you will complete the job in about half an hour. Super-size your mower to a 42-inch (1.07 m) riding mower, and you can mow the same plot in fifteen minutes. (This doesn't take into consideration bagging or mowing around obstacles, which takes more time.)

Buying a mower is not much different from purchasing a car. You might scour advertisements and review consumer ratings magazines to learn about the latest and greatest. What's on the market? You talk to your neighbors, ask them how they like their machines. Perhaps you quietly comparison shop while walking the dog, noting whether everyone but you cuts their grass with a ride-on mower. Or, maybe you don't want to spend more than your mortgage on your first mower. Each of us has different expectations, budgets, and requirements.

We visit a dealership or mass retailer with some idea in mind of what we ought to buy—or, at least, what we want. But our wish lists are often littered with priorities that have little to do with a mower's quality of cut. Instead, consumers tend to focus on horsepower and size—the testosterone of a mower.

Many homeowners approach a mower purchase with one of two mindsets. They want an inexpensive machine that will do a quick-and-dirty job: cut the grass. Or, they want all the bells and whistles that their neighbors have—and more. Neither considers what features they need to cut their specific lawn nor whether they plan to do more than just mow with the equipment (plow snow, haul materials, or aerate turf, for example).

Both consumers will likely be disappointed after operating their mowers for some time. Cost-driven purchases must be replaced when a homeowner realizes the equipment is too small for the job or won't support attachments that fulfill work requirements such as plowing snow. For example, a zero-turn mower (a mower that can turn 180 degrees or more) will mow large, flat properties efficiently, but don't expect to run attachments on these machines.

"The number one reason consumers buy a certain mower, now, is because of a recommendation from a neighbor, friend, or family member," says Mike Ballou, product manager of consumer and commercial equipment for John Deere. "That may not be the best answer for them. They really need to take a look at their needs."

The lesson: research; ride before you buy; and carefully consider your own requirements before purchasing a mower.

Q: I'm having a hard time steering my riding mower. Any ideas?

A: First, check your tire pressure. You could have a flat. Also check the front tie rods, which connect steering to the front wheels. If you hit something while mowing, you can disturb the rod.

—TROUBLESHOOTING WITH MIKE BALLOU,
Product Manager of Commercial and Consumer Equipment at John Deere

The Right Mower Match

Following are some questions to ask before you make an investment.

1. How large is your property?
Mower size is not everything, but a larger machine will help you cover more ground faster. If your property is an acre, or more, a lawn tractor or zero-turn mower will get the job done quickly. However, if your yard is the size of a postage stamp, a walk-behind mower is all you need.

2. What is the layout of your lawn?
Survey your property. Are the trees close together? Do you have to mow around plant beds or squeeze through fences? Answer these questions before you purchase a mower. Measure tight spaces. Determine the size of your storage area. Your mower should fit these space requirements and allow room to spare.

3. What is your terrain like?
Is your lawn on a slope, or is it flat and wide open? Is your turf pitted with ruts and bumpy areas? If so, you probably should refer to the first chapters of this book, in which we discuss turf amendment. You can improve your terrain so that mowing is safer and easier.

4. Who will operate the mower?
Before you purchase a mower, try it out. If you share mowing responsibilities with another member of your family, include this person in the decision. Your mower should be comfortable to control, and the only way to know this is to go for a test ride. A servicing dealer will offer this option.

5. Do you plan to use your mower for other tasks?
If your maintenance responsibilities include plowing snow, hauling materials, or performing other lawn care projects (tilling and aerating), you will want a mower that can multitask. Attachments available for riding mowers make this style versatile for homeowners with a long list of maintenance chores. On the other hand, if your sole task is mowing, a walk-behind or zero-turn machine will fit the bill.

If you plan to use attachments, you should consider horsepower in addition to mower style. You need more oomph to pull a cart or push snow. You'll also want a heavier-weight machine and a sturdy frame.

6. Where will you store the mower?
A mower is a significant investment, so protect it from the elements. Whether you plan to store the mower in your garage or a garden shed, measure the space before you make a purchase.

Quality Cut Construction
The truth is, most mowers on the market today accomplish the basic goal of mowing—making tall grass short. But not every mower delivers a high-quality cut, and most consumers don't know which mower features dictate how their grass will look. Although horsepower and deck size are popular selling points, you probably don't hear much about frame integrity, discharge shoots, or deck depth. This trio gets the credit for cut quality.

Welded Frame Construction: Look for a fully welded frame for durability. These machines are more solid than others, stand up to frequent use, and last longer.

Wide Discharge Chute: Clippings disperse more evenly from a wide discharge shoot.

Deep or Tall Deck: When mower blades turn, they create a vacuum effect in the deck. The suction pulls up grass, so the mower blades can make a clean cut. The taller the deck, the more space there is for grass to stand straight. When the deck is too shallow, grass bends underneath the deck as blades cut or gets "blown down," or flattened.

How Much Horsepower?

How much power you need depends on the type of work you plan to perform with your mower. You'll need less to mow flat ground and more to pull a utility cart or move up a hill with a bagger attachment. So, function is the first consideration when determining how much horsepower is enough.

There are three types of power:

- **Horsepower:** the raw power an engine can produce
- **PTO horsepower:** the power that an engine actually sends to do the work
- **Torque:** the rotational force that can move loads

You'll notice these terms in the operator's manual or features displays when you shop for mowers. Again, depending on what functions you want your mower to perform, your power needs will vary. First decide on the attachments you plan to use—the product information should list their horsepower requirements. Your machine should be equipped to manage their weight. Another point to consider is gasoline consumption. Naturally, the more power your mower puts out, the more gas it sucks.

The Right Mower Match

Keeping in mind the questions you answered earlier regarding your terrain and property size, as well as your true power requirements, you can now choose a mower that meets your needs. Following are some various property scenarios and the mowers that provide the best cut for each.

Scenario 1

The Property: You live in an urban setting and can cross your lawn in ten steps. Most of your back yard is consumed by a brick patio or courtyard, except for a frame of grass no wider than 5 feet (1.5 m).

The Best Cut: What looks like an antique is actually quite convenient for homeowners with tiny lawns—postage-stamp lots you could probably cut with a string trimmer. Until the 1960s, manual reel mowers dominated the market; their gas-powered counterparts were considered a luxury, and the technology came with a price. The advantages of a manual reel mower start with the ability to mow at a moment's notice. However, you must mow regularly, because this tool doesn't handle overgrown grass well. These mowers are best for flat surfaces.

Urban dwellers with quaint lots and small garages can choose this type of mower and not sacrifice storage space. Because these mowers operate on people power, they don't contribute to air pollution.

TODAY, YOU CAN PURCHASE lighter-weight aluminum reel mowers. They are the least expensive option.

Look for a rear-wheel-drive, walk-behind mower if you plan to use a bagger attachment. When mowing on a slope, a bagger will weigh down the back of a mower, causing the front to pop a wheelie and result in an uneven cut.

VERSATILE WALK-BEHIND MOWERS allow operators to address challenging areas without compromising the quality of the cut.

at various price points at retail home and hardware stores. Horsepower and engine size dictate price; deck size ranges from 21 inches (53.3 cm) to larger, 36-inch (91.4-cm) models. Self-propelled mowers require more horsepower than push mowers but also make the job easier if you must manage hills or if your property is on a slope.

Scenario 3

The Property: You live on several acres of property, and you want an efficient cutting solution. You like to aerate your own property, rather than hiring a professional landscaper to do it, and you enjoy taking on weekend outdoor projects. You're looking for a less labor-intensive method of cutting your lawn.

The Best Cut: Riding mowers and lawn tractors (their well-equipped cousins) cut large areas in less time than manual or walk-behind mowers. If your property is more than a ½ acre (1,000 m²) in size, you may consider one of these options. Operators with physical limitations also prefer riding models. An array of attachments allows you to convert these cutting machines into landscape helpers—snow plows, aerators, leaf collectors, you name it. (These attachments are generally sold separately.)

Scenario 2

The Property: You live on a ¼-acre (1,000-m²) lot, and your backyard is populated with trees. Your property is expansive, but plant beds and tight spaces don't allow room for a large riding mower. You want a quality mower, but your standard yard doesn't seem large enough to justify a tractor-sized purchase.

The Best Cut: Power rotary mowers feature a bar-like blade that rotates in the mower deck. These are the masters of maneuverability—ideal for mowing tight radiuses, between beds and around other landscape structures. This is also the most popular type of mower on the market today, and you'll find an array of brands

RIDING MOWERS are available in a range of sizes. Bigger is not better! Choose the horsepower and engine size appropriate for the tasks you plan to accomplish with the mower.

Q: What's the difference between a riding lawn mower and a lawn tractor?

A: A riding mower is designed to just cut grass. It generally features less horsepower and a smaller deck size. Lawn tractors are multipurpose mowers that can pull attachments and help with tasks like aerating, tilling, or hauling materials. You can also push snowplows or pull leaf-collection systems with a lawn tractor. To decide which is best for you, determine whether you truly need a multitasking machine.

Scenario 4

The Property: Your property is flat, with few obstructions, such as trees. Your lot is a couple of acres (0.8 ha), and you're looking for a sure, fast cut—clean and simple. You've watched landscape companies run mowers that finish the job in record time, and, admittedly, you like to purchase the latest and greatest.

The Best Cut: Zero-turn mowers turn on a dime and are ideal for properties of at least 2 acres (0.8 ha) in size, though you'll see homeowners and landscape companies operating them on ½-acre (1,000-m²) lots. The advantage of zero-turn riders is speed; they range from 19 to 30 horsepower. If you're shopping for testosterone, this is your machine—and ZTRs (zero-turning radius), as they're called in the landscape industry, are an increasingly popular pick for the homeowner market.

ZTRs accept a limited number of attachments, but a bagger is one that will fit. The downside to ZTRs is terrain: tractors handle slopes better than ZTRs. Also, some operators require time to learn how to run ZTR machines. Their steering is different from a traditional wheel. (If you know how to operate a twin-engine boat, you'll be familiar with how the twin-lever steering control works. For example, when the right steering lever is pushed all the way forward, and the left one is pulled all the way back, the mower will turn left.) But most people get the hang of it quickly, and find that these machines turn easily, move efficiently, and are fun to operate.

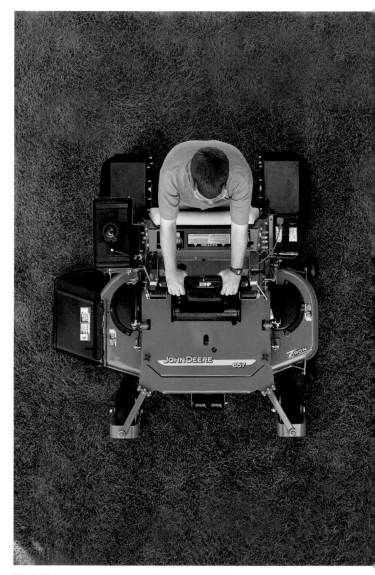

TRADITIONALLY A COMMERCIAL PRODUCT, zero-turn mowers are now available in lighter-duty models designed for consumers.

Accessorize Your Mower

You can outfit your mower to manage almost any landscape task. Attachments give your mower the extra appendages, if you will, to bag leaves, plow snow, aerate turf, till soil, haul materials, grade uneven turf, and fertilize your lawn, among other chores.

Plan for Power

Before you purchase a mower, determine what attachments you think you'll use. Certain heavy-duty implements require extra power. If you just plan to use a bagger, which often comes standard with a mower purchase, you don't need to invest in a supercharged engine. Plan for extra power if you know you will eventually want to dedicate tasks such as plowing and aeration to your mower. Most equipment literature includes charts listing the attachments each mower model can handle. If you can't locate this information at the point of purchase, ask a sales assistant or call a servicing dealer.

Start with Standards

Many walk-behind mowers come equipped with a bagging attachment. If yours doesn't, this will probably be your first attachment purchase. You'll appreciate the bag attachment in the fall. Also, if grass is especially long, collecting clippings in a bagger prevents you from having to rake the area later—or worse, leaving heavy clippings on the turf, where they might cause damage.

Add a Cart

Homeowners who garden frequently or enjoy do-it-yourself landscape projects will appreciate the cart attachment, which hooks up to a riding lawn tractor. Carts take a load off the operator, whether you are transporting flats of annuals from a front-yard bed to the back or hauling mulch or paver material.

Service Points

Just as you change the oil in your car every 3,000 miles (4,828 km), so too does your mower require regular maintenance. How you change it—by doing it yourself or by taking your car to a dealer or quick oil change station—is up to you. The same applies to mowers. If you care for your equipment by tending to seasonal maintenance needs, you will maximize the life of the equipment, ensuring that it operates at peak levels and delivers the best cut possible. If you skip out on annual oil changes or don't bother to sharpen cutting blades—well, don't expect the results you see in magazines.

Most current mowers are built so that you can easily access parts that need care on a regular basis. These are called service points. Depending on mowing conditions and frequency of use, your equipment may not need new blades or an oil change more than once each season. The time to do this is before spring.

Homeowners generally take their mowers in for service right before they plan to cut their lawns for the first time, after storing the equipment all winter. The problem with this plan is that dealers are swamped in the spring. You can expect to wait as long as six weeks if you put your service off until the last minute. If you do not plan to perform seasonal maintenance yourself, take your mower to a servicing dealer during the winter. Some dealers offer service specials, to encourage customers to think about service during the snow season. Take advantage of these! You'll save money, and your mower will be prepared in time for spring.

YOU CAN PURCHASE A COVER for your mower to protect it from dirt and debris. Before purchasing a mower, decide where you will store it, so you don't buy equipment that is too large for your space.

Service before Storage

First, let's talk end-of-season care. Before you store your mower for winter, remember these service points:

- **Drain the gas** from the fuel tank, and run the mower until it stops.
- **If you choose to keep gas in the mower,** add a fuel stabilizer, but do not do this without first checking your owner's manual.
- **Drain and properly dispose of the oil,** replacing it with fresh oil.
- **Remove the spark plug,** and lubricate the cylinder by pouring a drop of oil into the spark plug hole, then turn the crankshaft or pull the starter rope to rotate the engine and distribute the oil.
- **Replace the spark plug,** but don't reconnect the wire.
- **Clean dirt and debris** from the mower and underneath the deck.
- **Store** in a clean, dry place.

IT'S A GOOD IDEA to keep an extra set of sharp mower blades on hand, in case you need to replace them mid-season. Changing them takes less time than sharpening them.

Service before Spring

If your mower was in hibernation all winter, you'll need to prepare it for the cutting season by tending to the following service points. Some of these tasks overlap with winterization—how much you'll need to do in the spring depends on whether or not you took care of business in the fall.

- **Clean or replace the air filter**
- **Change oil***
- **Replace the spark plug***
- **Reconnect the spark plug wire**
- **Ensure that bolts by the wheel base are tight, and grease these points**
- **Sharpen mower blades**
- **Inflate tires, if necessary**

*Perform these tasks if you did not already do so in the fall.

Service Safety

Often, we are in a hurry to cut our lawns and move on with our programmed lives. But when maintenance is a rush order, accidents happen. Don't speed through gas fill-ups or oil changes. Whether you're simply filling up your mower with gas or performing an all-out winterization ritual on the equipment, you should keep in mind these important safety tips.

- **Never run the engine** while the mower is in the garage or an enclosed space.
- **Never add fuel** while the engine is running or hot.
- **Refuel your mower outdoors,** where there is plenty of ventilation.
- **Read instructions carefully** on fuel packaging, and refer to your owner's manual before filling your tank.
- **Wipe up fuel spills**—you don't want to start a fire.
- **Always, always shut off the mower** and disconnect the plug wire before performing any type of service.

SHARPENING BLADES does no good if you don't balance them. You can do this by hanging the mower blade from a nail pounded into a wall, preferably in a garage or shed. A blade that falls to the right or left is not balanced and indicates that you shaved too much from one side. You'll always be in balance if you take blades to a dealer for sharpening. The cost is generally inexpensive, and if you have a set of back-up blades at home, you won't miss out on mowing time while you wait a week for the service.

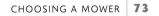

Routine Maintenance and Mowing

Whether you consider mowing a chore or a hobby, it is probably at least a weekly routine. But there is more to mowing than making tall grass short. Here, we present a mowing master class. Prepare to mow, deal with variables such as turf type and terrain, and avoid the common pitfalls that sabotage the quality of the cut.

Mowing is one of the cornerstones of routine lawn maintenance, and it plays a significant role in turf health. The right cut will promote growth, discourage weeds and disease, and protect the soil from losing moisture.

You'll also gain surface benefits. A fresh cut is the most obvious sign that you care for your property—no one wants to be the neighbor with the unruly turf. So we approach the job of making tall grass short with a certain pride. A carpet of painstakingly manicured turf is a suburban status symbol. And when the grass is greener on the other side of our property lines, we feel a pang of guilt that we aren't making our best impression. Call it green envy.

Accomplishing a master cut requires technique, attention to timing, and a knowledge of your turfgrass. There is an art to proper mowing, along with a great deal of science, but that doesn't mean the job is best left to professionals. With a few rules of thumb and the right equipment (see Chapter 5), you can establish an appropriate mowing routine that won't consume your entire day.

ANATOMY OF YOUR MOWER

GET TO KNOW YOUR MOWER. With a basic understanding of the equipment components, you'll be a safer, more productive operator.

Mechanical Mower Engagement Lever

Steering Wheel

Throttle Choke Lever

Transmission Shift Lever

Key Switch

Mower Deck-Height-Reminder Tab

Attachment Lift Lever

Blade Control

Fuel Level Window

Deflector Shield

Reverse Travel Pedal

Cutting Deck

Forward Travel Pedal

Rope Start Handle

Grass Bag

Oil Fill and Dipstick

Fuel Filler Cap

Real Height Adjustment Lever

Spring-Loaded Recycling Cover (Raised Position)

Front Height Adjustment Levers

Never operate mowing equipment with the discharge chute raised, removed, or altered, unless using a grass catcher. This chute is designed to reduce the chance of thrown objects.

THE DISCHARGE CHUTE plays a dual role. It helps to evenly disperse grass clippings, and it directs foreign objects toward the ground.

Time to Mow

Although a weekend afternoon might be the most convenient time for you to mow your lawn, it doesn't mean your turf is prepared for the ordeal, especially if you recorded inches of rain on Friday night.

For safety and turf-health reasons, don't mow when the grass is wet. Break the routine, and give yourself the day off if grass is wet and slippery. Less traction can make equipment difficult to handle, and you are more likely to lose control while mowing even gentle slopes. Also, your turf will not appreciate the burden of heavy machinery when the soil is wet. Wheels mat down turf and leave visible tracks. These stressed areas will not allow sunlight to penetrate through the turf. Diseases thrive in dark, wet places, especially weak areas.

It is also important to avoid mowing after sundown. Operating a mower at night is like walking blindfolded. You are likely to overlook debris or obstacles and not notice a protruding tree root or garden hose. Wait to mow until daytime, when you can see nature's roadblocks and any people or animals that might cross your path.

THE RIGHT HEIGHT

HOW LOW SHOULD YOU MOW? The primary rule is to cut off one-third of the turf plant at one time. Whether you have just returned from vacation to find turf gone wild or you mow religiously every few days, the same rule applies. Your goal is to maintain the recommended height for your lawn and avoid giving your turf a crew cut.

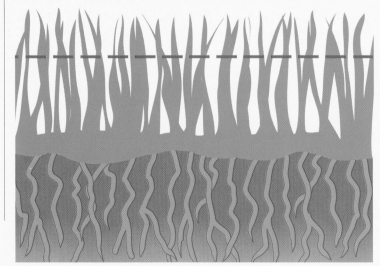

The recommended height for your lawn varies with turfgrass variety. Most grasses thrive when cut at 2 to 3 inches (5 to 7.6 cm) in the fall and spring. Set your cutting deck higher in the summer, so grass can soak in the sun, allowing it to grow and develop. Always mind the recommended cutting height for your turfgrass variety. For example, if you live in Florida and your lawn is St. Augustine grass, turf height should range from 2½ to 4 inches (6.4 to 10.2 cm). Following the one-third rule, if your lawn is 7 inches (17.8 cm) tall, you should remove a little more than 2 inches (5 cm) at one time.

Q: My mower is making strange vibrations. I don't understand.

A: The deck is usually the source of vibrations. Chances are, you hit something while mowing and set your mower blades off balance. To find out for sure, first turn off the mower and disconnect the spark plug, to prevent injury. Look underneath for debris. Once the deck is clear, start the mower to listen and feel for vibrations. If you still hear unusual sounds and rumbling, the problem might be internal, perhaps in the engine. This is the time to call your dealer or reliable service center.

—TROUBLESHOOTING WITH MIKE BALLOU,
Product Manager of Commercial and Consumer Equipment at John Deere

Precut Prep

Before priming your mower and turning the key, you'll want to make a few adjustments. When you rent a car, you probably check the side mirrors and adjust the seat, to get acquainted with the controls and avoid getting stuck in a downpour without knowing how to turn on the windshield wipers. Whether your mower is brand new or an old standby you just uncovered from winter storage, it's always a good idea to review your operator's manual, to get reacquainted with your machine. Refer to the maintenance check sheets on pages 72–73 in Chapter 5 to prepare for the season.

Deck: A level mower deck is one of the keys to a clean cut. You can level your deck in a couple of different ways. One simple method starts with ensuring that your machine is on a flat, level surface. Lower the deck to the 2-inch (5-cm) cutting height position. With a tape measure or ruler, measure the distance between the blade to the ground on the left and right rear sides of your mower. If they are not equal, turn the leveling nut on each rear lift link (refer to Anatomy of a Mower illustration). The front of the deck should be ⅛ to ¼ inch (3 to 6 mm) lower than the rear corners. Another way to check if your deck is level is to lay a 2-by-4 under the deck. Lower the deck onto the 2-by-4, and you will see whether or not the sides are even.

Seat: Adjust the seat on riding and zero-turn mowers, so you can comfortably reach the controls.

Safety Controls: Read all safety instructions, and note the warning labels visibly posted on equipment. Understand how to disengage mower blades, safely mow in reverse, and stop in an emergency. (It's a good idea to review your safety manual periodically.) Test controls regularly.

Fuel and Oil: Add oil and fuel only when the engine is cool. Do not smoke while fueling, and, to avoid carbon monoxide poisoning, do not start the mower in an enclosed area.

Clean Sweep

Clear the mow zone of all debris. Children's toys, mulch bits, rocks, and branches can catch in mower blades and get stuck under the deck, causing a temporary breakdown. Even worse is the risk of thrown objects. A rock becomes a safety hazard when propelled at 180 mph (290 kph) from a mower deck. A simple spot check of your property before mowing can prevent these hazards. Also, trim low-hanging branches that might interfere with mowing.

Each year, 25,000 people are treated in U.S. hospitals because of injuries related to riding mowers. To youngsters, especially, lawn mowers look like large toys, and they don't understand the danger of rotating blades. Review safety information with the whole family, so everyone understands that mowers are for adults only. Ask children to stay indoors while you mow.

Recommended Mowing Heights

TURF VARIETY	MOWING HEIGHT RANGE
Bahia grass	2 to 4 inches (5 to 10.2 cm)
Bermuda grass	1 to 3 inches (2.5 to 7.6 cm)
Buffalo grass	2 to 4 inches (5 to 10.2 cm)
Centipede grass	1½ to 2½ inches (3.8 to 6.4 cm)
Fine Fescues	1½ to 2½ inches (3.8 to 6.4 cm)
Kentucky Bluegrass	1½ to 3 inches (3.8 to 7.6 cm)
Perennial Ryegrass	1½ to 2½ inches (3.8 to 6.4 cm)
St. Augustine grass	2½ to 4 inches (6.4 to 10.2 cm)
Tall Fescue	2 to 4 inches (5 to 10.2 cm)
Zoysia grass	1¼ to 3 inches (3 to 7.6 cm)

A Tall Order

The one-third rule is a guiding principle for several reasons. First, you want turf to develop a deep root system, so it can capture moisture and shade the earth. When you cut grass too short, you remove leaf material (the green color)—the photosynthetic area. The plant can't grow and recover as fast, and the result is brown turf.

Second, taller grass is stronger, denser, and healthier. When you give your turf a buzz cut, you thin your turf's protective reserves and risk weakening the root system. Finally, too-short cuts promote aboveground shoot growth, rather than healthy, deep root growth. Strong roots are the plant's anchor, and when the proper cultural practices discussed in the first part of this book are used, those roots will help ensure a healthy lawn, year after year.

Stay Sharp

Think of your mower blades as you would a set of good steak knives. When they're sharp, they make a clean cut, and carving an attractive main course is effortless. Sharp mower blades deliver the same neat finish. Having sharp blades also means you'll mow the lawn faster, because cutting through the turf takes less effort. Finally, sharp mower blades shred turf into finer clippings, which break down quickly and feed the turf with organic nutrients.

How often you sharpen the blades depends on how often you cut and whether you follow that one-third rule. Naturally, frequent mowing wears down blades—heavy use causes more wear and tear. But if you cut off locks of grass, rather than an inch or two (2.5 or 5 cm) at a time, turf will collect in the mower deck and force blades to work harder to do their job. Your soil type can also have an affect on blade life; sandy southern soils, for example, are abrasive and gradually file away blades. In general, sharpen or replace blades each spring, before the heavy mowing season. Check them periodically, according to your mowing habits, to see if they need more attention.

Switch Directions

If you mow toward the street one week, mow toward your home the next. Change mowing patterns and directions on a regular basis. Grass has a tendency to lay the way you mow it. When you alternate mowing directions, turf stands at attention, and you achieve a cleaner cut. Also, you'll avoid telltale lines from wheel damage and resulting turf wear.

ALWAYS BE SURE your mower is turned off, the sparkplug wire is disconnected, and children are clear of the area while changing mower blades. You may want to wear safety gloves during this process.

Bag, Mulch, or Discharge?

First, let's address a common myth concerning the bag-it-or-leave-it debate. Mulching turf as you mow *does not* cause thatch build-up, which is a proliferation of dead grass and roots that can become a barrier to water and fertilizer if it accumulates. Mulching will not choke your lawn if you follow the mowing practices discussed. Because grass blades are 85 percent water, they will eventually dissolve into the turf canopy. The rate at which they dissolve depends on the temperature, moisture, and length of clippings. Dissolved clippings feed nutrients back into the lawn.

But there are a few ifs to mulching. Mulching is good *if* you cut only the top-third of turf, *if* grass is not heavy and wet, and *if* it is not fall.

MOWING WITH A GRASS COLLECTION SYSTEM will save you hard labor come leaf-raking time.

So how do you decide whether to bag, mulch, or simply discharge clippings into your lawn?

Season: In the fall, you want to remove leaves from your lawn, so you can apply fertilizer before winter. Bagging is the best way to do this. You can use a grass collection system, which looks like a couple of garbage cans, that attaches to the mower; a lawn sweeper (also a tow-behind attachment); or a basic bagger that attaches to a walk-behind mower.

Otherwise, you can rake leaves in the fall, to remove them from your lawn. In spring and summer, mulch turf or allow clippings to discharge onto the lawn.

Turf Length: Do not mulch if you cut off more than one-third of the turf at one time. Grass will clump and sit in wet clods on your turf. Clumps will smother your lawn if you don't pick them up after mowing. Mulching is ideal if you cut in layers, a little at time, allowing thin grass slivers to fall into the turf canopy and decompose as nature's fertilizer.

Compost: If you plan to compost your clippings, you'll want to bag them, so you can easily transport them to a designated bin. Otherwise, you must rake clippings and collect them manually.

LAWN SWEEPERS feature rotary brushes that gather leaves into a bin.

DO NOT ALLOW GRASS CLUMPS to collect in the mower deck. This will affect your quality of cut.

NOTICE THE MULCHING PLATE on the left side of this mower deck. When it is in place, your mower will not discharge clippings but will, instead, mulch them by slicing up the grass blades and dropping them back into the lawn.

Technique: Tricky Situations

If every lawn were as flat as an airport runway and as smooth as artificial turf, without a bump, berm, slope, or sharp corner in sight, the pros would have nothing to brag about. Mowing a straightaway is simple. But maneuvering over some of today's modern, suburban landscapes just isn't that easy. Our properties are obstacle courses in their own right. Plant beds, trees, drainage ditches, even gradual grades can present a challenge when mowing.

Here's how to conquer the tough spots.

Corners: Zero-turn mowers turn on a dime. Riding mowers round out curves. Walk-behinds are maneuverable and fit into tight spaces. Take corners slowly, so you don't tear up turf while turning. If a tight angle compromises your safety, use a trimmer in that area, or choose a walk-behind for closer control.

Trees: When mower wheels are forced to round a tight radius, they can dig into turf and damage it over time. You can achieve a clean cut around trees by first using a line trimmer to cut grass close to the perimeter. Follow up with your riding or zero-turn mower, making a wider circle around the tree.

NOTICE THE STRIP that edges this flower bed. You may wish to install similar edging, so your finished cut looks more polished.

MANEUVER SLOWLY AROUND
BEDS—take your time! You may want
to conquer these tough spots first
before tackling the rest of your lawn.

Beds: Many of today's riding and zero-turn mowers
are designed to manage tight spaces. Base your choice of
mower size on your property's restrictions, so you can
mow between beds and around landscape structures
without a problem.

If you must mow between two beds that don't allow
room for equipment to pass through, consider using a
walk-behind mower or trimmer for the job. You might
want to use a four-wheel steer mower, which provides
great control and stability around trees and plant beds.

Slopes: The way to test whether you can mow a slope
with a riding mower is to attempt to climb the slope in
reverse. If you cannot back up the hill, you should not
mow it with a riding mower. If you can reverse up the
slope without a problem, you can then mow it carefully
in forward gear. If you can't back up the slope, then mow
the area with a walk-behind.

A WALK-BEHIND MOWER provides complete
control when mowing next to beds. In addition
to giving you a better view of the cutting area,
a walk-behind easily squeezes into tight spots
and manages sharp corners.

Q: My riding mower is stubborn and just won't start. What's the deal?

A: First, make sure your mower blades are not engaged. A safety device prevents you from being able to start the machine with rotating blades. Next, check that your brake pedal is engaged. Also, if you are a petite operator, the mower may not recognize that you are sitting down. Some roll-over-protection systems are activated by a sensor in the seat. If the mower thinks no one is in the seat, it stops, to prevent blades from turning if you fall off. You may not be heavy enough to deactivate this sensor, which means the mower won't start. Talk to a servicing dealer about making an adjustment.

—TROUBLESHOOTING WITH MIKE BALLOU,
Product Manager of Commercial and Consumer Equipment at John Deere

When using a riding mower, be sure to travel directly up or down the slope. Because weight distribution is different with zero-turn mowers, you should mow across the slope. Likewise, mow across slopes when using walk-behind mowers.

When mowing a slope, avoid sudden stops or turns. Mow slowly, and always look behind you when moving in reverse. Mowing with a grass catcher on a slope will affect your stability. Consider front weights to improve balance. When towing any load—on flat surfaces or up and down slopes—do not allow the tow weight to exceed the combined weight of machine, operator, and any ballast used. Remember, the distance required to stop increases with your load weight. When mowing a hillside, the extra weight magnifies this equation. Mow with care. Slopes are not ideal terrain on which to use mower attachments, because gravity already compromises mower control.

YOUR RIDING MOWER can cut around trees, but consider trimming the area first, so you can make the turn without missing turf closest to the tree bed.

BIGGER ISN'T ALWAYS BETTER. If your property features a maze of plant beds, or your lot is heavily wooded, consider a walk-behind or compact riding mower.

Finishing Touches

The process of finishing your work—trimming and edging, pruning, and cutting back stray tree and shrub growth—is much like coloring within the lines of a pencil drawing. If you carefully outline the edges and follow the curves and

Take time to maintain the shape of shrubs, to edge your lawn, and to keep stray tree branches trimmed back. These finishing touches enhance curb appeal significantly—it's the little things.

angles of each shape, the result is a polished, thoughtful design. Scribble outside the lines, or avoid them all together, and the work looks disheveled—not complete, just colored in.

A freshly mowed lawn deserves attention to its edges. Consider this your finishing class. Don't cheat by avoiding precision practices. The time you spend polishing your work won't go unrewarded.

There's something about a clean finish—a polished edge—that differentiates an OK lawn from an eye-catcher. There's something about an even line, rather than a ragged perimeter, that marks a mowing job well done. That something is edging and trimming, the icing on the cake, in terms of lawn maintenance.

Your yard may be half-baked from dry weather, and the turf variety might not be the best quality. There's always room for improvement. But if you tidy the edges, a sense of order and uniformity will likely overshadow any marked deficiencies in your lawn. This is not to say that edging and trimming negate the lawn care practices we've been doting over for the past six chapters. Rather,

compare these finishing tasks to the chores a clean-up crew manages to perform in a large stadium. A grandstand might look impressive, jammed with interesting people, food, and action (in landscapes, think plants, flowers, and features). But if there is trash laying around, the impact sours. The view is a letdown. Trimming and edging your lawn are easy ways to create a manicured impression—and they are not that difficult.

Let's call this clean-up work "finishing." Trimming and edging work applies to the perimeter of your lawn, bed edges, and areas where sidewalk meets turf and grass meets your home's siding. Trimming is also necessary for maintaining shrubs and smaller trees that may require cutting back for safety or aesthetic purposes. Acquiring proper equipment and knowing how to operate it safely are prerequisites for these practices. Here, we'll cover the when, how-much, and how-often questions pertaining to finishing practices.

Clean Edges

Trimming and edging are purely aesthetic practices. Unlike amending soil, irrigating, or applying fertilizer, trimming and edging won't improve the actual health of your turf. Sure, it will prevent creeping grasses from growing outside the boundaries you set for your lawn, but its purpose is mostly curb appeal. Still, make a couple of wrong moves with a trimmer, and you can create turf health problems. For example, if you get too carried away with the string trimmer, you'll likely scalp the turf—never a good idea. And if you give shrubs a crew cut, you risk removing leaves that are necessary for growth and regeneration. When trimming, edging, or pruning, adopt the mantra "less is more."

There's a difference between edging and trimming. Most homeowners use these terms interchangeably, but they are entirely different activities.

Edging is a vertical cut. An edger usually has a metal blade that cuts into turf like a knife, creating a definitive line between turf on one side of the blade and the surface on the other side (pavement or mulch). Edging is usually performed monthly—just a few times each summer, if your lawn is a cool-season grass. Frequency always depends on your turfgrass variety.

Trimming is a horizontal cut achieved by a string trimmer, more casually known as a weed whacker. (You won't hear lawn care professionals call it that, though.) The head of a string trimmer resembles a hockey puck with two plastic whiskers. Trimmer line, as the string is called, is usually rounded, though some brands offer line with bladed edges. The trimmer head spins at high speeds, and the string cuts through turf leaves, tearing and whipping down the grass. String trimmers are rudimentary machines, and they come in various sizes and styles (curved or straight shafts).

Trim your lawn after every second mowing. If you choose to trim every time you mow, don't trim too much of your turf. The optimum trim height should be equal to your turf height—not shorter. A common mistake homeowners make is to lop off a border of grass that makes the edge look like it's a step down from the rest of the lawn. Avoid this temptation. Trim edges so they are even with turf height. If you mow at 3 inches (7.6 cm), edge at 3 inches (7.6 cm), for a seamless finish.

CAREFUL TRIMMING provides a rectangular effect in landscapes like this one. But you better be prepared to keep up with maintenance. Perfect angles look messy when you allow stray growth to take over.

Trimming Tools

The equipment you choose to edge and trim your lawn will determine the results. You can use a string trimmer to edge your lawn, but its whipping action will not dig along the perimeter of your property to remove unwieldy turf. A stick edger will get the job done. Many homeowners purchase one piece of equipment—a string trimmer—and use it for both practices. You can clean up edges with this tool, but you won't get a defined edge. Also, to treat a string trimmer like an edger, you must position it so the line rotates in a vertical direction. This means you are running the equipment while holding it an angle and operating it for purposes beyond its core application, which is simply to trim stray grass.

STRING TRIMMERS are two-cycle machines that use a whipping motion to cut grass. They are designed for trimming around trees, along bed edges and lawn perimeters, and in areas that mowers cannot easily access.

An edging machine has a blade that digs and cuts into turf. The blade's slicing action cuts away gnarly edges. Stick edgers are close cousins to string trimmers, except a circular blade attachment replaces the spinning trimmer head. A stick edger is a more compact version of an edging machine and is easier to store than traditional edgers, if garage or shed space is a concern.

NOTICE HOW THE OPERATOR scoots this edging machine along her sidewalk to slice off unruly edges. Eye protection is always recommended.

Attachments allow homeowners to assign trimming and edging tasks to one piece of two-cycle equipment. Simply change the head to an edging blade or rotating trimmer head to accommodate the task at hand.

Purchase Pointers

The variety of string trimmers and edging tools available on the market caters to every type of home lawn. Consider the size of your property, your standards for the finish, and your budget. Two-cycle equipment can be relatively inexpensive, and there are several reputable brands available in retail stores that will last for years. Make a list of how you will use two-cycle equipment, which includes string trimmers, stick edgers, hedge trimmers, and pole pruners (used for both tree and shrub care).

Ask yourself the following questions before making a purchase.

- **What size** is your lawn?
- **Will you be the main operator** of the equipment, or are your purchasing it for use by another person in the household?
- **Do you prefer** gas-operated or electrical equipment, and what is your power availability?
- **How much** would you like to spend?

First, let's address where to find a quality piece of two-cycle equipment. If you purchase commercial-grade trimmers and edgers from a dealership at which landscape professionals shop, you'll know the equipment is built to last. In fact, these machines are designed to operate day-in and day-out in conditions far more stressful than those on your property. If you choose to buy equipment from a dealer, rest assured, he or she will offer maintenance instructions and direct you toward the appropriate type of trimmer line and oil.

On the other hand, because an array of equipment is available at retail stores, you can probably find two-cycle equipment in the aisle next to the mulch or patio furniture. Most mass merchandisers stock equipment models that range from bare-bones to professional-grade—but don't settle for the bargain bin price. As with anything, you get what you pay for. Choose one of the major brands. There are several reputable names on the market, and their equipment is comparable. If you have questions, ask a servicing dealer for his or her thoughts on which machine best matches your needs. Finally, avoid the temptation to purchase power. Engine size is not important, but versatility, sturdiness, and reliability are.

Now, let's return to the previous questions, starting with the size of your lawn. If it's the size of a postage stamp, you can probably get away with an electric string trimmer that plugs into a garage or exterior outlet. These light-duty machines are effective for small areas that require limited use, and they are convenient for homeowners who don't want to mess with a gas-oil mix. The downside is dealing with a cord, which can pose an obstacle during operation. Also, trimmer line for electrical machines is usually thinner, often coming out of only one side of the trimmer head, unlike the two feeds of line on most gas-powered trimmer heads.

Gas-powered string trimmers, also referred to as two-cycle equipment, require mixing oil and gas for fuel. This is a relatively basic process. (See The Right Mix on page 92.) Two-cycle equipment is ideal for mid- and large-sized properties—wide, open spaces and areas to which a cord won't reach and would surely get caught by plant beds and other landscape features. Two-cycle trimmers and edgers are the most commonly used, and they are just as easy to operate as their electric counterparts. The benefit of two-cycle is flexibility and power, or tenacity to whip away denser grasses.

Finally, consider who will operate the machine. Each brand and model of equipment feels different, so it's important to have the main operator handle the equipment before purchasing it. Is the shaft (handle) the right length? Is it comfortable to hold the equipment? Is it too heavy, or does it feel awkward? As with cars and motorcycles, features are designed to accommodate various types of operators. For example, if you are petite, a curved handle may feel more comfortable. Meanwhile, a straight shaft will extend your reach for trimming stray grass in discreet places, such as underneath decks.

Weeding out which piece of two-cycle equipment is best for your job can be overwhelming. If you don't know where to start, pick up one of the several available consumer ratings magazines. These are solid references to consult if you want third-party feedback on equipment performance.

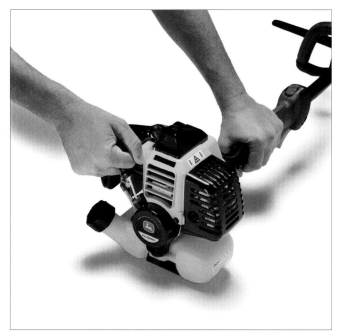

A QUICK PULL on the starting cord is all it takes to rev up two-cycle equipment like this string trimmer. When starting the engine, you should position it on a flat, bare surface, as pictured.

Equipment Care

Dealers often receive phone calls in the early spring from frustrated homeowners saying they can't get their string trimmers to start, no matter what. What could be the problem? Dealers can diagnose this trouble without thinking twice. Many times, homeowners leave two-cycle mix in the tank all winter long. They lay their equipment to rest after the growing season but do not drain the fuel or run the equipment dry. The result: a no-start come spring. Does this sound familiar?

Two-cycle equipment can outlive your car if you take care of it properly. This means investing in quality oil, properly winterizing equipment, and purchasing quality trimmer line.

Drain and Run Dry

Following the last time you use a piece of two-cycle equipment for the season, you must drain the gas/oil mix and run it dry. First, call a local dealership or your municipality and ask about proper fuel disposal. You cannot simply throw away this mix—you can't pour it in the corner of your yard that your neighbors can't see, and you can't drain it down the sink. This is absolutely dangerous and harmful to the environment. If you do not want to spend the time and energy to seek out an approved fuel disposal site, then take your equipment to a dealer for end-of-season service.

After properly disposing of fuel, run the equipment dry. Pull the starting cord and turn on the trimmer, then let the machine run and eventually stop. This way, you know the tank does not contain leftover gas/oil mix, which clogs lines when equipment sits for months without use. Starting two-cycle equipment that sat all winter, full of fuel, is like feeding it sludge. Don't expect it to perk up.

Trimmer line comes in different shapes and sizes. Size is indicated by diameter—how thick the line is. Lighter line is used in electrical trimmers, while heavier line is required for two-cycle equipment. Check your user's manual to find out what type is recommended for your equipment. Also, you can purchase line that is rounded or has bladed edges, which will slice through the grass. Bladed line works well in heavier-duty applications.

The Right Mix

When using two-cycle fuel, be sure to mix the gasoline and oil according to the ratios provided in your equipment owner's manual. You should also read the back of the oil packaging for mixing instructions. You can also purchase fuel in easy-to-use, premeasured packages. For best results, purchase top-end oil that is labeled for the equipment brand you choose. It pays to spend a little more for a better-quality oil.

To avoid confusing lawn mower and two-cycle equipment fuels, keep two separate gas containers in your garage or shed. Distinguish them with marker or colored tape, or purchase different colored containers. The same organization is beneficial if you own several pieces of two-cycle equipment that require different gas/oil ratios.

Feeding Fresh Line

You probably won't need to change trimmer line more than a couple of times a season—maybe less. The process is not complicated, but following these steps will help make the process trouble-free.

1. Purchase the correct size of trimmer line for your equipment. Check your owner's manual for specifications. (Sturdier .095 line will last longer than .065. These numbers indicate the thickness of the line in inches.)

2. Stop the engine and push in the locking tabs to release the trimmer head. Remove the stringhead cap from the base, and remove the spool.

3. Unwind excess trimmer line from the spool.

4. Cut a length of line approximately 25 feet (7.6 m) long. Fold the string at the halfway point, leaving one half about 3 inches (7.6 cm) longer.

5. Place the loop around the notch in the spool.

6. Hold the spool and neatly feed trimmer line by rotating the spool. Do not wind the line around the spool, which could cause it to tangle or wind unevenly. Look for an arrow that indicates the direction in which to wind line onto the spool.

You can never be too careful when using hand-held equipment, because the risk of thrown objects is great. Think about it: rotating blades and line meeting turf. There is a possibility that a trimmer could whip up debris, along with clippings. Keep small children indoors during operation, and make sure to clear the area of branches and the like. If you are trimming along the edge of a sidewalk, turn off the machine for passersby, so you don't put them at risk, too.

Always wear eye protection when operating string trimmers, edgers, or any sort of hand-held equipment. Hearing protection is also suggested when operating equipment that produces noise of 85 decibels, or more, and most gas-powered lawn mowers and string trimmers exceed this level.

7. When finished, snap the string ends into the notches on the edge of the spool, leaving about 4 inches (10.2 cm) of string hanging beyond the slot. Be sure there is no trimmer line trapped underneath the spool after snapping it shut.

8. Place the spool and line back into the stringhead cap, pulling the trimmer line through the slots in each side of the cap.

9. Push down the cap until the locking tabs are secure. Be sure the trimmer line is not trapped and the assembly is secure by advancing the line manually before operating the equipment.

Shearing Shrubs

You've seen what an overzealous homeowner with a hedge trimmer can do to a shrub. A little trim here, a shave there, a bit more on the side, might as well even take off the top. Before long, the slightly overgrown plant, now naked and leafless, is a skeleton of its former full-bodied self. Don't count on a quick comeback from a scathing trim job. Leaves lend shrubs regenerative powers, so without them, your shivering shrub will maintain its close-cut look for quite some time. Regrowth depends on the shrub variety, but the lesson here is the same for trimming and edging: Less is more.

Another rule to remember when trimming shrubs is to aim for a natural effect. Select individual stray branches and clip them carefully with hand shears or pruning shears.

Examine the shrub for the following:
- **Unruly growth**
- **Weakened or dead branches**
- **Disease-infected branches and leaves**

Remove this growth and take a conservative approach to trimming the rest of the shrub.

Remember, shrubs don't grow with perfectly flat tops, and they don't mature into neat squares or circle shapes. (Although some homeowners who want to achieve a topiary look or symmetrical landscape design may intentionally create shapes from bushes.) If you want a tidy shrub that doesn't look sculpted, your best bet is to use manual tools to snip away branches, instead of electric or gas-powered hedge trimmers. The temptation with power hedgers is to sweep the trimmer across the top of the shrub. It's too easy to overtrim this way. Simple hand pruners or shears will help you accomplish the same task in moderation.

On the other hand, large jobs and neglected shrubs with an excessive number of overgrown branches deserve the precision and speed a powered hedge trimmer can provide. And using this type of equipment will require less energy and time.

THESE HAND SHEARS AND PRUNERS are ideal for clipping back shrub growth.

THESE MANICURED SHRUBS feature a sculpted look.

BENEFICIAL TRIMMING

Trimming shrubs is beneficial to plant health because it improves light penetration, allowing sun and air to circulate. By removing dead, weakened, and disease-infected branches, you prolong the useful life of the plant. Proper trimming promotes growth, discourages disease, and improves the appearance of shrubs.

Tree Trimmings

Trees are tricky business, mostly because trimming branches can require a ladder, heavy-duty equipment such as a chain saw, and safety equipment that most homeowners do not own. For these reasons, consider calling a professional, rather than managing tree trimming yourself. The risk of injury when performing this type of work is much higher than when simply trimming shrubs. If you must climb up a ladder, operate a chain saw to cut through a branch, or remove several branches and/or an entire tree, turn the job over to a pro.

If you want to clip back a dead branch on a young dogwood no taller than a teenager, then go ahead. You can manage the size and scope of this project by using a pole pruner, which looks like long-handled hand shears. If a storm leaves dead branches hanging from trees, you can cut back those within reach, to prevent a safety hazard. Then call a professional to manage the rest. You can also avoid the area completely and hire a tree care specialist to clip back dead branches. Tree care is a specialty, and you'll find services that focus on this type of maintenance. Trees are a subject in the school of lawn care, because their needs are complex, and the care required can involve dangerous equipment and risk to the homeowner. Trim shrubs yourself, but call in the crews to manage the big guys.

Smart Cuts

Ideally, only cut tree and shrub branches that are 2 inches (5 cm) or less in diameter. Cutting branches greater than 4 inches (10.2 cm) in diameter can potentially result in decay. Make a thinning cut by removing the branch back to the parent branch or tree trunk. This type of trimming reduces the size of the tree canopy and lets in sunlight and air without damaging the tree. Thinning cuts will also reduce the weight that branches bear, decreasing the chance of breakage. Thinning cuts are made mostly on shrubs and trees that are middle aged and older.

MAKING THE RIGHT CUT

REDUCTION CUTS are appropriate when pruning larger branches, 2 inches (5.1 cm) in diameter or larger. Do this by making cut #1 on the underside of the branch. Cut halfway through and stop. Make cut #2 on opposite side of the branch, 1 inch (2.5 cm) further in from the first cut. Make this cut until the branch falls off. You will be left with a shorter, more manageable branch. Angle your final cut #3 downward, away from the trunk, and be sure it's beyond the tree collar.

THE BRANCH COLLAR is where the trunk and branch overlap. In many species, the collar is obvious by a subtle bulge in the branch that looks like a joint. Cut beyond the branch collar. (Leave that collar on the tree.) This will prevent tree injury during pruning.

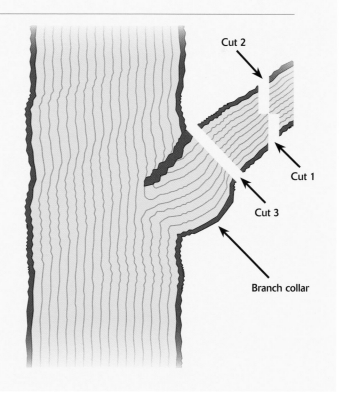

Cut 2

Cut 1

Cut 3

Branch collar

Q: When is the best time of year to trim trees and shrubs?

A: Light pruning (less than 10 percent of the tree or shrub canopy) can be done all year, but the best time to prune is when plants are dormant during the winter. During the spring and summer, trees and shrubs are under stress, as they flower and develop leaves. When you prune them at this time, you give them even more of a workout. They must recover from the pruning while dispensing energy to bloom and grow. So, if possible, keep pruning to times of the year when trees and shrubs are less active and, therefore, more likely to heal successfully from wounds caused by shears or clippers.

—MARK A. SCHMIDT, ADVANCED RESEARCH
and development for John Deere, discusses tree and shrub care techniques.

Most homeowners who live in urban neighborhoods do not need a chain saw. They are potentially the most dangerous piece of equipment on the market, and the risk of injury for inexperienced users is significant. They are messy, loud, and require skill to operate. Of course, with proper training and safety gear, chain saws are an effective way to cut wood, remove large branches, and perform other hardware tasks. They are irreplaceable tools for certain heavy-duty applications. But most of the time, these same tasks can be accomplished by a landscape or tree care professional without you having to invest in the equipment or worry about proper gear, such as chaps to protect legs from thrown objects. Chain saws are more often used by homeowners in rural environments, where there is plenty of open space and less risk of thrown objects harming others or damaging property.

CHAIN SAWS ARE POWERFUL cutting tools, and you'll find various styles designed for reaching high into tree canopies. Called pole saws, these are generally used by professionals. You'll notice this operator is wearing a helmet, gloves, chaps, and ear protection.

THE HOMEOWNER using this chain saw on his rural property wears jeans to protect his legs from debris.

Clean-up Crew

After edging and trimming, the final touch to a mowing job is to remove clippings and stray debris from sidewalks and driveways. The best tool to manage this job is a blower, and you can choose from a couple of different types. A backpack blower is nice for larger spaces, and the ergonomic style puts less of a burden on your body if you are blowing leaves or using the machine for a hefty job. Available in electrical or gas-powered options, hand-held blowers are an accessible, quick clean-up tool to finish off a job well done.

BLOWERS CAN KICK UP DIRT AND DEBRIS, so it's wise to wear eye protection. Pictured is a backpack-style blower.

Noise regulations in some communities dictate when, how, and what type of blower you can use. Find out whether your city has restrictions which might include limitations on what time you can operate blowers (not too early in the morning). Most blowers sold in the homeowner market run at acceptable noise levels.

HAND-HELD BLOWERS are versatile and easy to store.

PART THREE

Weekend Workshops

Now that you have the tools and knowledge to care for the foundation of your property—your turf, the canvas—you can begin infusing your landscape with design elements that personalize the space.

Dream big! Build your ideal outdoor living room, one project at a time. Included are weekend projects to help you maintain your lawn and ideas to enhance your property with water features, lighting, and pathways.

PROJECT

Aerate Your Lawn

Fall inspires a list of clean-up projects, and aeration always tops the charts. For many homeowners, the process is a rite of passage, a symbolic process that signals preparation for season's change. By lifting from the turf vial-sized cylinders of soil that can clog root development, you clear the way for a hardy spring. Out with the old, in with new growth.

The signs are there at the end of every summer season: flyers from landscape companies advertising aeration services; signs in your local lawn and garden store announcing aerator rentals; telling soil plugs in your neighbor's lawn. The leftover dirt droppings from an aeration job can make a mess—and for what?

Many homeowners buy the service, or perform it themselves, without realizing why, other than the fact that their neighbors do it. Or, they feel that aeration is a fall rite of passage, even if they don't understand the importance of this annual end-of-season turf health practice.

What exactly is aeration?

As the name implies, aeration is a process that airs out the soil. It serves two main purposes: alleviating compacted soil and cultivating soil in a mildly disruptive way. The practice is performed by a rather heavy piece of equipment called an aerator or by an attachment with similar mechanics that fits onto a riding mower.

Aerators use a series of hollow or solid tines to puncture the ground and pull out soil cores. (Solid tines actually poke holes without removing soil, but this action serves the same purpose as core removal: decreasing soil volume.)

Removing soil cores improves the water-oxygen exchange in the soil and alleviates compaction. Com-

AERATION WILL HELP this lush, green grass stay healthy.

Not sure whether you need to aerate? Go ahead and unplug your lawn—it certainly won't hurt, as long as you aerate when the grass is least stressed out. For cool-season lawns, fall is the best time. If your turf is Bermuda grass or another warm-season variety, plan on renting an aerator or signing on for the service from May through August. Warm-season grasses repair more quickly from mild agitation in the summer, when they are strongest.

paction is high-density soil and is counterproductive to root growth. When the soil is packed tightly, roots can't push through, and the turf plants weaken. Aeration cleans out the soil's clogged pores and prepares the turf for new growth in the spring.

The process is easy and monotonous—no more complex than mowing a lawn. You certainly don't need to hire a professional for

NOTICE the compacted roots in the center and far right turf plugs.

aeration services, though you may choose to, if you do not want to spend the time or rent the equipment to do it yourself. If you prefer to rent the equipment for a day, you can split the reasonable price with neighbors who might also want to aerate their lawns. Why not get the most use out of the machine?

You'll learn some techniques to ensure you make the most of your aeration here, but first, you're probably wondering: Do I really need to aerate?

Why Aerate?

Soil compaction and minor turf agitation are the key reasons to aerate your lawn. Compaction occurs slowly over time, and, without paying close attention to turf growth, you may not detect the visible clues of compacted soil. If your lawn endures heavy foot traffic and you mow at least weekly (and you probably do, especially during the growing season), chances are, you're gradually packing down the soil. Feet work like tampers, and equipment bears weight on the soil. Neither pressure is fatal to turf, but these stresses will have a negative affect on grass roots if you don't create some breathing room for them. As roots grow full-throttle in summer and consume every available space underground, your soil becomes dense and impervious to oxygen and water—not a healthy situation.

The signs that your turf needs to be aerated are often subtle.

Spotty Turf Areas: Compacted soil prevents root systems from developing. In extreme cases, you might notice bald areas in your lawn where the turf has died out. You also might see patches where the grass isn't as dense.

Matted-down Grass: Compacted soil tends to retain moisture longer—too long, in some cases. Roots can begin to rot, and the result is a weak turf plant that might not stand up straight.

Sparse New Growth: Weak roots and turf don't fill in to become a dense, lush carpet of grass. Compacted soil chokes roots and cuts off their oxygen and nutrient supply. You can't expect new turf to grow strong in this type of environment.

Pools of Water: In severe cases, you'll notice pools of water collecting on your lawn and that moisture does not easily absorb into soil. These are signs that the lawn is compacted and does not have pores to soak up water.

Tough Ground: Can you push a screwdriver or similar tool into the ground easily, or do you feel like you're driving metal into rock? If the latter is true, you had better aerate.

Aeration alleviates these symptoms—the process is both curative and preventive. Curative, because aerating your lawn removes cores of weak turf and roots, so you can overseed the area. And preventive, because you clear the way toward establishing a healthy, fresh turf canopy for the next season. If soil is compacted in the fall, and you do nothing to open its pores, the problem will only worsen when spring ignites turf's hormones (in cool-season grasses). Ripe for growth, roots will have nowhere to spread, and your turf will not get the head start it needs before it must endure a summer of heat and stress. So, why aerate? You put more pressure on soil than you realize, and unclogging its pores once a year is necessary to help your turf breathe, and to clean out the tangled mess of roots that can develop under the surface. That way, you can make room for fresh, new growth.

Room to Grow

Mild agitation from aeration actually heals weak turf. Think about how your muscles respond after a strenuous gym session. The pressure you force on your muscles when working out with weights actually tears muscles—though not in a bad way. (Unless you overdo it, and in aeration, the same rule of moderation applies.) Now, consider what happens when you take a rest day after your work out. Muscles repair, and new tissue develops to fill in those torn spots. Every time you break down muscle, your body builds it back up—bigger

and stronger. Plant life is remarkably similar, in that removing soil cores—breaking up the ground—allows room for new roots to grow in and support healthy turf.

It is important to prevent those soil plugs from being squashed back into the ground. You negate the positive effect of aeration when plugs are pushed right back into the soil—and it can take a few weeks for them to disappear naturally. It is best to stay off the lawn following aeration. Your lawn mower can cut up dried plugs and return nutrients and nitrogen to the soil (your shoe treads will probably collect some of the plugs, too), but the best way to ensure that turf plugs won't reclog your turf, especially if you plan to overseed or topdress your lawn, is to rake them up. This is quite labor intensive, however, and the reality is that most homeowners won't follow up aeration with this chore. Let's face it: A total keep-off policy is nearly impossible if you plan to maintain your lawn. Just try to limit foot traffic.

Postaeration is the ideal time to renew a scrappy-looking lawn. Your soil is turned up and more accepting of fresh seed. Now porous, the soil has room to add vital nutrients to your lawn in the form of compost, ground peat, and sand. Rake a light layer of this mixture (topdressing) over your lawn, and you will reestablish a soil profile that encourages healthy turf. You can add extra seed to your lawn after topdressing with organic material. If your lawn is bare in some spots because of compaction, you might want to seed it; early fall is the best time to do this, so seeds can germinate and establish before winter.

A CAVEX RAKE can be used to dethatch small lawns.

When renting equipment, always ask for an operator's manual and read it carefully before digging into your project. When you use a machine only once a year, you'll probably forget how to operate it from year to year. Brush up on how to start and operate the machine, and learn how to shut it off in case of emergency. Ask the renter/retailer to give you a quick orientation on using the equipment. A quick lesson before reviewing the operator's manual is always a good idea.

Aerate or Dethatch?

Dethatching and aeration are similar, in that both processes agitate the lawn and break up soil and turf to promote healthier growth. Because both involve machines with tines, the practices are easily confused. But there is a distinct difference between the equipment used to remove thatch and to core aerate a lawn, and the processes remedy different weak-turf symptoms.

Dethatching, also called verticutting, is a slicing action whereby a series of vertical blades rotate and slice into turf. Dethatching pulls up dead and dry remains of turf roots and plants that lay underneath healthy turf in a visible, brown carpet. This layer of thatch prevents water, oxygen, and nutrients from reaching the soil and turfgrass roots. You can easily detect thatch. If your lawn looks two-toned in spots—straw-like turf remnants sitting underneath healthy sprigs of green grass—then thatch is the problem.

Dethatching is generally a more aggressive practice than aerating. A single pass over a lawn with a dethatcher will interrupt the reproductive cycle of turfgrass plants in the spring. Avoid dethatching or aerating in summer or when the turf is under stress. For warm-season grasses, do not dethatch or aerate when turf is dormant. Your yard will not properly recover from the tine agitation, and you'll end up with a lawn that's in worse condition than before you started.

Areation can remedy light thatch coverage, because the unplugging action of the tines naturally removes dead underlying turf, so, if you have compaction and light thatch problems and want to use only one practice to solve them, choose core aeration. A single pass of an aerator over your property won't damage your lawn.

Before You Begin

While aerating is basically a no-brainer project, a couple of preparatory tasks will make the job much easier. First, consider the moisture level of your soil. Avoid aerating when soil is dry and hard as concrete—the tines will need to push harder to pierce the ground, and you'll overwork the machine. Aerate your turf in the fall, when the drought season has passed, the soil is moist, and the tines will more easily enter the ground. But keep in mind—while moist soil makes aeration easy, sopping wet soil just makes it a muddy mess.

Another preproject consideration is temperature. Again, fall is the best time, because cool-season grasses are generally not battling extreme heat. You don't want your turf to be under temperature stress during aeration. This is like forcing someone to run a marathon in sweltering heat—don't expect peak performance. Likewise, turf won't bounce back from agitation or accept nutrients and seed as readily when it is too busy expending energy to stay alive in hot or dry conditions. Keep this in mind when you decide what day to rent your aerator.

Finally, be sure to mark irrigation spray heads, pet tie-ups, and other stakes or fixtures in the ground that an aerator could damage. Aerator tines are unforgiving. Irrigation heads probably won't survive the grueling, puncturing force of tines.

Remove all debris, including fallen branches, from your lawn before aerating, and wear eye protection, in case of potential thrown objects during operation. In most applications, sunglasses can double as safety goggles.

Step-by-Step Aeration
THE SUPPLIES
- **Lawn rake (for removing debris)**
- **Core aerator machine**

THE STEPS

1. **Be sure your lawn** is at the right moisture level and temperature for aerating. If necessary, water your lawn the day before, so you don't overwork equipment by forcing tines to drive into rock-hard soil.

   Most core aerators are self-propelled. Make even passes across the lawn, as if you are mowing the area.

2. **You may choose to rake** up cores, to avoid squashing them back into the lawn, or you can allow them to dry up, allowing the material to return to turf and serve as a valuable nitrogen and nutrient source. The less foot traffic on your lawn following aeration, the better.

3. **Be sure to water** your lawn after aerating. Creating pores in the soil allows water and oxygen to enter the ground—give your lawn a good soak, so roots can drink up moisture and begin the rebuilding process.

Create Bed Edging

Edging creates a neat border—a boundary, a framework, the finishing touch—on a landscape bed. Edging tames plants, so they stay where you put them. It holds together the intricate patchwork of color and texture in a bed and defines a space as special. In addition to the functional aspect of edging, the variety of materials you can use to outline and polish bed edges adds a new dimension to your outdoor living space.

Edging is an affordable way to outline the shape of beds and polish planting areas. Not only does edging lend a neat-and-clean look to any landscape, it also

serves many practical purposes. Edging prevents creeping plants from overstepping their boundaries and overflowing into turf areas. It also serves as a barrier that keeps soil and mulch contained in plant beds. Should rain or wind threaten to disperse material into the lawn, edging will trap soil in place. Edging prevents turf roots from invading planting areas and reduces your maintenance responsibilities—scratch trimming scruffy turf edges off your list!

Most of all, edging creates a transition from turf to beds. For homeowners who want to achieve a manicured, linear landscape, bed edging is a fast, budget-wise practice that results in a high-impact finish.

LANDSCAPE BEDS WITHOUT EDGING, such as this one, have a free-and-easy look about them—they're less linear and more wild looking. Depending on the style of your outdoor living space, a less manicured look might be appropriate. However, this bed would benefit from edging material, which would highlight the curved shape of the space and follow the theme set by the topiaries behind it.

The materials available to accomplish this range beyond the basic plastic strips traditionally associated with edging. However, this option is convenient because it conforms to curved or straight edges and is relatively inexpensive, compared to hardscape materials such as decorative concrete pavers. In this chapter, we'll show you how to install plastic strip edging, the most common edging used. You can apply the steps to install most edging, no matter what style you choose.

Get Inspired!

Today's landscaping market is well equipped with a variety of edging to suit any taste. You'll find surfaces that meld with nature, such as stone and decorative concrete pavers. Fashion-forward selections allow you to leverage the overall design of the living space. Price varies depending on the material, and the most affordable option is the black plastic mainstay. Keep an open mind when shopping for bed edging, and consider options that coordinate with the surface of your home.

Materials Matters

Take a tour around your neighborhood. How do other homeowners edge their landscape beds? You can gain ideas by honing in on finished projects—and spying on the people who live nearby. Notice the difference between raised plant beds with retaining-wall edges and beds that are level with the turf surface. What style will complement your outdoor space?

Consider your landscape design and the existing surface materials of your house, patio, and other features when choosing edging. Available is a palette of materials designed to add interest to your space, including the following:

Plastic: Black plastic strips come in rolls and easily accommodate curved or straight beds. You can also find plastic pieces that resemble mini-fencing and stake into the ground.

Composite: Composed of recycled post-consumer waste, composite has a natural-grain wood finish and, like plastic edging strips, can be manipulated. The material won't splinter, crack, or rot and is virtually impervious to insects and moisture.

Concrete: Precast concrete comes in a variety of shapes and sizes: scalloped or pointed edges, traditional square or rectangle shapes, and even molded seashells. (See photo on page 115.)

✎ **DESIGN TIP**

Choose edging material that works with the shape of your landscape bed. Don't plan on shaping metal to create the curvature of a half-moon. Each material has limitations, so talk to a store professional about appropriate options before investing in a product.

The installation method for plastic edging applies to most materials. Find out if the material you choose requires special treatment.

Metal: Metal edging is a heavy-duty, long-lasting solution for an industrial/contemporary look and for beds containing rock or other heavier materials that require a sturdier border to keep them in place. Metal is also ideal in commercial applications. Although metal edging seems to be catching on in the south, as well as in regions in which gravel is prevalent in landscape beds, it's less popular in northern climates. It is best used to edge straight-lined beds, as its malleability is limited.

Wood: Wood planks and railroad ties blend well into wooded lots, but be sure to treat the wood before installation, so you don't encourage weed growth or invite insects to nest in it. Using vertical wood cylinders arranged in varying heights or trimmed to the same length to edge beds is another approach.

Live: Finish edges with hedging, annuals, or other grasses, to create a transition between

the lawn and landscape bed. Mondo grass, an evergreen perennial with short, glossy dark-green leaves, is a popular border because of its low-growing, spreading characteristics.

Before You Begin

There's nothing like instant gratification—starting an outdoor project on a Saturday afternoon and finishing it in time for a backyard barbecue the same day. Won't your guests be impressed! Most of the projects in this book are easily managed in a weekend or just a short afternoon of work. But the key to

THESE SHELLS ADD A DECORATIVE TOUCH, serving as ornaments to dress up the bed as much as barriers to keep soil land plant life from bleeding onto the adjacent paver surface.

IF YOUR HOME IS BRICK, consider carrying out the theme in your landscape by using diagonally placed bricks as a border. These can serve as a neat trim for pathways and plant beds.

FOR A NATURAL LOOK, incorporate interesting rocks as edging to a bed or ornamental grasses. Large rocks create a smooth transition between this barn garden and the rock path.

efficiently completing any project, including edging installation, is to prepare for the task. Take time to account for measurements, materials needs, and tool requirements. And always remember to plan for extras, just in case (extra edging *just in case* you fall short, a professional to whom you can turn for help *just in case* you run into a roadblock). Accounting for the just-in-case factor will save you time in making second and third trips back to the store.

Speaking of planning, consider the disaster you could create if you dive into a project such as bed edging without mapping out your ideas. You dig a trench for edging, for example, then realize that the bed isn't shaped the way you want it; in fact, you'd rather redesign it to create a divider between your property and the neighbor. Well, now that you have a trench in the shape of a half-moon, looks like you've got some filling and replanting to do.

If you didn't measure—and remeasure, *just in case*—the perimeter of the bed, your trip to the retailer to purchase edging might be the first of many, as you realize, midway into the project, that you are several feet short of material.

Consider where you will dispose of the dirt and turf chunks you remove during installa-

tion. Some municipalities do not permit the disposal of green waste, which means you'll need to compost the material or take it to an approved dumping site. You'll also want to use a wheelbarrow or garden cart to remove dirt and turf leftovers from the site.

Finally, take into account timing, the main obstacle to getting the instant gratification you might expect with a simple project such as bed edging. Working against Mother Nature only makes the job harder. For example, if the weather is dry and the ground hard, don't expect to easily drive in stakes to stabilize edging. And if it rains heavily after those stakes are in the ground, they can shift. The best time to edge is when soil is moist.

Before beginning a bed edging project, take care to do the following:

- **Be sure the bed** is located where you want it. If you choose to redesign the size or shape, do this before digging the trench for the edging.
- **Measure the perimeter** of the bed. Then measure it again.
- **Base your choice** of edging material on your style and the bed's contents, shape, and size.
- **Ensure that the ground is soft,** so you can easily dig a trench and drive in stability stakes.
- **Gather the tools** necessary to complete the project.

Step-by-Step Bed Edging
THE SUPPLIES

When choosing tools, shop for function and comfort. Consider your size and height—compatibility counts. You can find tools in various handle widths and pole heights. (Also look for comfort grips.)

For this project, you'll need the following:

- **Flat-edged shovel or edging tool**
- **Hand spade (optional)**
- **Rubber mallet or hammer and piece of wood** (for tapping in edging stakes)
- **Plastic bed edging and landscape stakes**

Be sure plastic strip edging is securely staked and stable in the ground, so it doesn't rupture when frost contracts the soil. Set the lip of the edging so it hugs the ground. That way, edging will stay in place while you are mowing close to the edging. Also, keep in mind that stakes are easiest to drive into the ground when soil is somewhat moist. If the weather has been dry, wait until the ground softens up after a rain before installing bed edging.

THE STEPS

1. Measure the perimeter of the bed, and double check your figure for accuracy. You don't want to run out of materials and waste time making extra trips to replenish supplies.

2. Unroll plastic bed edging, measuring and cutting it to fit the size of the plant bed. Allow a few extra inches for a seam to avoid a gap in the edging. You can trim away excess edging after completing the project. It's easier to cut off extra than to add on edging to fill a gap.

3. Prepare a trench, using an edging tool or flat-edged shovel (spade). Dig alongside the bed, piercing soil and turf on a diagonal angle.

4. Place edging in the trench, and firmly press landscape stakes into the ground, to secure the lip of the edging to the surface.

5. Finally, using a rubber mallet, tap in the stakes, to ensure they are secure in the ground. You can also place a piece of wood on top of the stake and tap the edge with a hammer, to force the spike into the ground. (Using a hammer alone to tap in edging can damage the edging material; it's also less awkward.)

6. Once edging is in place, fill the space by pressing soil into any gaps in the trench.

PROJECT

Cover Ground

If your yard has areas in which growing grass is troublesome, using a blanket of groundcover is an unexpected way to color landscape surfaces. Whether uniformity is your style or a mish-mash of flowering plants better suits you, a slew of varieties and creative expressions using groundcover will inspire you to treat it as a focal point, not just a space filler.

Turf is the most popular groundcover, and we've dedicated this book to telling you how to establish the very best. But sometimes it doesn't work out. Some areas are stubborn, and just won't allow turf plants to establish. Perhaps your property has patches under shady trees, which do not provide enough sunlight for grass. Or maybe you've tried for years to care for turf on a slope, only to have bald patches and erosion to show for it. Many of our properties have spots that are too shady, too sunny, too sloped, too difficult to mow, or too susceptible to foot traffic, which destroys even the most vital lawn. Remember the rule about putting the right plant in the right place? Turf isn't always the right plant. Sometimes it's best to use another type of groundcover.

These groundcovers do far more than color in the blank spaces in your backyard portrait. They provide texture, add interest to properties with extensive lawns, serve as interesting transitions between planting areas, and create lovely beds for taller trees. Groundcovers stop erosion and send a "keep off" message to pedestrians. If you want visitors to follow a path, plant groundcover on either side of it—they are not likely to stomp through it. (Turf is another story!)

For some homeowners, groundcover's most attractive quality is that it's low maintenance. Most varieties mature within two years, and, unlike turf, they don't need to be cut weekly. In fact, most groundcovers only require annually clipping back the outgrowth.

When installing groundcover, you'll apply virtually the same practices that you use to plant annuals or perennials in a bed. Proper plant selection and soil prepa-

ration will dictate your success. Before we show you the steps to installing groundcover, let's explore the benefits of turf alternatives and the design possibilities you can try as you plan your outdoor space.

A Healthy Alternative

Besides pure convenience, groundcover offers a host of health benefits to a landscape, especially the weak points in your property, such as those receiving insufficient water and sun. Groundcover can actually restore the ecological balance in your yard. It helps soil retain moisture and protects areas prone to erosion. Groundcover serves as a living mulch, reducing moisture evaporation and protecting the earth from unforgiving elements, including rain, heat, and cold.

The result is a fertile, welcome environment for a diversity of plants that otherwise might not survive. In a nutshell, it's groundcover.

- **Stabilizes soil**
- **Covers ground** in places in which turf won't thrive, such as shady areas
- **Provides low-maintenance,** seasonal interest—no mowing!
- **Creates texture**
- **Restores moisture** to soil
- **Prevents** soil compaction

A Garden Variety

Groundcover shouldn't be an afterthought in your landscape design. Some of the most interesting spaces feature creeping ivies, spongy moss, low-growing herbaceous covers, year-round evergreens, and woody ornamentals. Groundcovers can be showstoppers, adding texture and creating a three-dimensional canvas with layers of plant life. In fact, homeowners looking for an innovative way to landscape their property can turn to groundcover. It is often more dramatic and always more creative than turfgrass.

When choosing plants for your property, forget a couple of assumptions about groundcover—that it doesn't always lay low, and it isn't always green.

Groundcover refers to any vegetation that provides a dense, even cover—a plant carpet, if you will. This includes evergreen and deciduous plants, herbaceous and woody species, ornamental grasses, perennials, and annuals. A bed of impatiens serves as groundcover, as does a colony of hostas, or a collection of ferns. Carpet roses spread just as common ivy does, but their fragrant flowers and attractive foliage infuse a bed with color and scent. Explore groundcover possibilities with a nursery professional, who can offer suggestions on new varieties and insight on the types of groundcover that are appropriate for your property.

Beware of groundcover touted as fast growing or rapid coverage. "Quick coverage" can translate to "invasive." Find out exactly what type of plant you are purchasing, and ask a garden center professional for approximations of how for the groundcover will spread once mature.

When determining which plants to choose for your groundcover project, consider the following variables:

Groundcovers spread in different patterns. Popular groundcovers, such as English ivy, pachysandra, and myrtle, grow in a creeping motion, spreading and filling in bed space. However, ornamental grasses, which are also considered groundcover, can grow several feet tall before you cut them back in early spring to 8 inches, so they can start their cycle over. Balance the area by mixing shorter groundcovers with ornamental grasses.

Groundcovers vary in their need for sun. Take stock of your yard. Are areas shielded from the sun by trees or other structures, such as porch overhangs? Does the space get full sun all morning and sit in the shade most of the afternoon? Sun exposure determines which groundcovers will thrive in the bed. For example, common juniper likes sun, while lily-of-the-valley prefers shade. Pachysandra, which was planted as an example for this book, thrives in part to full shade. Ivy is also a hardy choice and grows well in partial shade. If you plant groundcover to fill in a shady area but choose a sun-loving plant, you'll only be frustrated when you experience no more success with groundcover than you did with grass in that spot. Base your choice of groundcover on the site's shade/sun quotient.

Groundcovers have soil requirements, too. Just because groundcover will spread and thrive in turf-resistant areas doesn't mean the soil in which it is planted is irrelevant. Soil quality is equally important for groundcover plants. You must prepare soil for planting (see Before You Begin on page 124), adding amendments if the soil lacks nutrients. It's not a bad idea to first perform a pH test to find out whether the soil is acidic, alkaline, or balanced. Offer this information to a nursery professional who can direct you toward varieties that will thrive. You may want to apply fertilizer to the area, to improve the soil pH. Most of all, understand that soil is home for these plants—if they are comfortable there, they will grow and maintain their vitality. Remember to amend, prepare, and take care of your soil.

Groundcovers might sleep during the winter. Herbaceous groundcovers can go dormant in climates that experience hard winters, and

GROUNDCOVER AS A TREE SKIRT

ROOTS ARE OBSTACLES FOR LAWN MOWERS, and grass doesn't always grow well under the shade of a tree canopy. Groundcover is a viable option to improve the look of this area. However, avoid planting groundcover around dogwood trees, which need good drainage to thrive. The constant watering required to establish plantings need is too much water for a dogwood. In particular, avoid planting annual groundcovers, which require water daily.

THIS PACHYSANDRA serves as a transition between the lawn area and taller plants in the bed.

PLANTING GROUNDCOVER in a curvy bed adds interest to an otherwise square yard.

annuals won't retain blooms year-round. Consider whether you want your space to show year-round color and interest. If you battle cold weather, choose evergreens or ornamentals with berries or seed heads. Ornamental grasses will turn brown but still offer texture and color during winter months. When shopping for plants, find out what they will look like when weather is at its warmest and after the first frost. Although a plant may not flower or stay green all year, its off-season characteristics can still be appealing.

THE DEFINITION OF GROUNDCOVER can be quite broad. In this case, an assortment of annuals and perennials works as groundcover. The homeowner chose a show of color, rather than a green lawn.

MOSS INFUSES A LANDSCAPE with a soft, green haze and an earthy appeal.

Before preparing the soil to plant groundcover, consider spraying the area with a nonselective herbicide to remove weeds and grasses. This treatment will remove stubborn grasses and other undesirables that your groundcover will eventually replace.

Before You Begin

After selecting the appropriate type of groundcover for your site, prepare your soil for planting. Often, the area in which you decide to grow groundcover does not contain the best soil. It might be dry from overexposure to sun or compacted from foot traffic. You'll want to loosen the soil, so the plants can easily take root. Work soil to a depth of 8 to 10 inches (20.3 to 25.4 cm), and incorporate a layer of organic matter, such as peat moss or compost. Sandy soils will benefit from amendments, which will help them retain moisture longer. This is especially important when establishing the groundcover bed—you don't want to lose water when feeding young plants. You might also want to add coarse sand to compacted soil, to improve its porosity.

Also an important factor is the soil in which the plants are potted when you purchase flats or 4-inch (10.2 cm) containers. Check it for wetness before taking them home. If the soil is dry, they might not have been watered regularly. The underdeveloped root systems of already stressed plants may not recover from neglect. Don't set yourself up for trouble. Stick your finger into the soil—it should feel damp to the touch.

Another fast way to stress out new plants is to set them in the ground in the heat of the summer. If possible, avoid planting at this time of year, and instead begin this project in fall or early spring. Allow plants enough time to establish roots, so they can bear heat stress during the dry months.

Step-by-Step Bed Edging
THE SUPPLIES

Planting doesn't have to be backbreaking work. Use a helper such as a garden cart, wheelbarrow, or even a riding lawn mower attachment for hauling flats of annuals or loads of potted plants. If your plants are very small and your soil is loose, you can hand-dig a hole, rather than using a trowel.

Following are some basic supplies you'll need to install groundcover:

- **Gardener's gloves**
- **Kneeler (optional)**
- **Steel rake (for turning up soil)**
- **Trowel**
- **Watering can or access to a hose** (for watering in plants)

SLIPPERY SLOPES

PLANTING GROUNDCOVER on a slope will prevent water run off and soil erosion, but vegetation doesn't fill in overnight. Be sure your soil is enriched with peat moss, so it traps as much water as possible before gravity takes over. If the slope is severe, throw down some annual ryegrass seed when you plant the groundcover. The seed will germinate within a week and, because it is an annual, will expire within one season. In the meantime, it will hold the soil in place, so plants can establish. The following year, the ryegrass will not grow back, and your groundcover will have matured and filled in the areas in which soil erosion and water retention were problems.

THE STEPS

1. Prepare the soil by turning up several inches and working in a layer of organic matter, such as peat moss or potting soil (for smaller areas). Then, smooth the area with a rake until level, being careful not to compact the surface.

2. Remove plants from containers and lay them out in a grid pattern, approximately 8 inches (20.3 cm) apart. If you place plants too close together, their roots will compete for water and nutrients, and the bed will become a game of survival of the fittest. While the area might look sparse in the early stages of growth, the groundcover will fill in the area and mature within two years.

3. Lift each plant from its spot and dig a hole in the soil, using a trowel or your fingertips.

4. Set the plant in the hole, and gently press down the roots, so they make contact with the soil. Repeat this process for each plant.

5. Water in the plants, ensuring that the soil is constantly moist for the first week after planting. Be careful not to overwater plants, which is just as harmful as allowing roots to go dry, or allow standing pools of water to form at the base of plants. You can ease off your watering schedule after the plants begin to take root.

Install Drip Irrigation

THIS PROFESSIONALLY INSTALLED drip irrigation head efficiently delivers water to a shrub area. You can install a similar water delivery system yourself.

Water conservation drives homeowners to experiment with drip irrigation. The pure efficiency of these systems is reason enough to install it in plant and flower beds, gardens, and other spaces in which trees and shrubs grow. But beyond water savings, drip systems deliver water to plants in droplets—manageable quantities that the soil can drink up in due time and deliver to roots. The result is less disease, a healthier plant, and less soil erosion and runoff. Ready to set up your own system? Easy-to-install kits make the project a snap, and you'll be thankful when you see your lower water bill.

You've probably seen drip irrigation in use without realizing it. Large farms use networks of drip irrigation piping to water row crops and orchards. Nurseries generally install a form of drip in irrigation greenhouses, where plants are carefully fed, so they can grow into saleable stock. In consumer applications, southwest desert communities adopted drip irrigation in their landscapes as a way to conserve water. Because water is scarce in these regions, homeowners depend on low-pressure drip systems as the most efficient way to water plants without waste from runoff or evaporation.

Drip is not limited to these applications, however. Although turf is best watered by sprinklers and irrigation systems, plant beds really benefit from drip systems. Consider drip irrigation as an effective watering alternative if your landscape includes garden spaces, trees, shrubs, or container plants.

Drip Delivery

The drip irrigation system used in this installation project looks like a hose with small holes that allow water to gurgle or mist (depending on the hole size) out of them. Water seeps from the tube onto the soil, which absorbs the moisture slowly. This gradual, slow watering promotes deep root growth and overall plant health. Hose-end systems are extremely versatile and can be staked into the ground, cut and split into sections, arranged along curvy beds, or snaked between areas with trees and shrubs.

Drip Benefits

When you douse plant beds with water from a garden hose, a puddle can form. Although the soil soaks up as much moisture as possible, hoses gush water, so the net effect is runoff—a stream of water that trickles along plant beds, down slopes, and wherever the soil is not protected by groundcover. Hose watering gradually causes erosion.

Because drip irrigation delivers water in small quantities through gentle misting or by droplets, the soil isn't bombarded with a high volume of water. This is important, because standing water will suffocate young flowers and plants. Submergence in water makes them more susceptible to disease.

Another bonus of drip irrigation is significantly less water waste, and conservation is especially important in communities that enforce water restrictions. When using a hose to water a plant bed, you may use as much as 400 gallons (1,514 L) of water per hour—far more than your soil will accept. And because sprinklers and hand watering deliver water to the soil surface, moisture is more susceptible to evaporation, resulting in more waste. Drip irrigation provides the deep-root watering that plants need to thrive. Soil absorbs water at the same rate that drip irrigation hoses deliver moisture.

In clay soils, water from sprinklers or hoses can actually compact the surface. When clay becomes too wet, it forms a mucky soup. Once it dries, the surface hardens and cracks in places where the water evaporated. Compact

DRIP BY DESIGN

IF YOUR LANDSCAPE includes any of the following features, drip irrigation is an ideal water delivery method.

- Plant and flower beds
- Container plantings
- Trees and shrubs
- Gardens
- Greenhouses

If you plan to go on vacation, or you want year-round, worry-free watering, install a timer on your drip irrigation system. You can purchase these á la carte and integrate them into your hose-end drip irrigation system. Program a watering schedule, and set applications for the best times of day: before dawn and evening, when the sun and heat won't threaten absorption.

soil surfaces in plant beds looks as though they were subjected to an earthquake; the ground is pocked, left with dried rubble and uneven areas in which the water formed puddles and forced the soil aside. To remedy the situation, any homeowner's natural response is to water more—bring out that hose. But the best watering system for plant beds with clay soils is drip irrigation, which will distribute water slowly and evenly, so it can penetrate the soil and reach roots.

Another point about root health: Plants that are overwhelmed by water don't get enough oxygen. Air won't reach roots if the soil is over-saturated with water. Because drip irrigation delivers water drop by drop, moisture won't displace oxygen, and the roots will receive both vital nutrients.

For efficiency reasons alone, homeowners should consider installing drip irrigation wherever possible. It is easy to install, and hoses that provide the slow, trickle action are widely available in home and garden supply stores. They are affordable, and you can retro-fit them to manage most planting areas.

Before You Begin

Drip tubing comes in different sizes, measured by *inside diameter* and *outside diameter*. If you are adding onto an existing drip system, be sure to purchase the correct size and parts, or buy a coupling system, so the tubing will fit. The hose-end drip system installed in this project is a kit with a soaker hose. The tubing is already punctured with holes, which eliminates guesswork. You might wish to use tubing that allows you to install emitters that distribute water. But for an annual or peren-

nial plant bed application, the soaker hose is an appropriate, easy-to-install option.

Before purchasing a drip irrigation kit, measure the area in which you plan to install tubing. You may need to purchase extra couplers or tubing if the kit does not contain enough to cover the space.

Step-by-Step Drip Irrigation
THE SUPPLIES
Drip irrigation kit, which contains:
- **Filter**
- **Backflow preventer**
- **Hose fitting**
- **Tee fittings and couplers**
- **Support stakes**
- **End fittings**

3. Attach filter and backflow preventer to the water source. If the water pressure is more than 50 psi (pounds per square inch), you'll need a pressure regulator.

4. Some kits contain emitters that allow you to control where the water will spray from tubing. Think of them as mini irrigation spray heads, except that they pop up from the tubing. Poke the emitter into the tubing, according to the instructions on the packaging. Be sure to align the emitters, so they deliver water to the desired plants.

THE STEPS
1. Measure and cut tubing to fit the area.

2. Fit tubing into elbow-shaped joints, which allow you to run a system along corners and to arrange tubing in a row formation for watering gardens or flower beds.

Create a Pathway

Pathways guide visitors through your landscape, drawing the eye to focal points and leading people from point A to point B. Whether your taste is contemporary, traditional, earthy, or Old World, you can manipulate various materials into a walkway. By using

curvy, straight, or geometrical designs, you can create a finish that's either clean cut or whimsical. Sharpen your skills by learning how to install a basic stone pathway—then let your imagination guide you and experiment with different surfaces.

Pathways are functional, as well as aesthetic. For practical purposes, they serve as dividers in a planting area and act as guides to lead visitors through the spaces you so carefully designed. In a design sense, pathways break up large areas into usable quadrants for garden-

ing, entertaining, or outdoor play. They also act as joints that connect landscape features, restoring order to a yard with a plant bed here, a pond there, a patio off to the side. By installing a single pathway, you can unify projects that once seemed like distant cousins, stranded in designated areas of your yard. If foot traffic is a concern, you'll save your turf from getting stomped on by installing a pathway that sends a clear signal to keep off the grass. You won't have to worry about muddy feet tracking into the house if you place stepping stones in areas prone to poor drainage.

Home and garden retailers sell an array of materials suitable for creating pathways—you can even make your own, by molding concrete into shapes. (There are kits to show you how.) The following project clinic will focus on how to create a stepping stone pathway.

Carving out a route from point A to point B isn't a difficult process, but it does require some forward thinking. Once you dig out a hole of turf to hold a paver, stepping stone, or other hardscape material, you leave a gap in your lawn. This spot will be artfully filled when you install the surface you choose—but if you decide that the placement isn't quite right, you're left with a bare spot.

Answer the following questions before deciding where to place your pathway.

- **What do you want visitors to notice** in your outdoor space?
- **To what features** must you travel before you can enjoy them?
- **Are there areas** in which turf growth is a problem?
- **Would alternative surfaces** here look more appealing?
- **Does your yard** contain landscape features that don't seem to connect?
- **If your turf was a moat of water,** what bridge would you need to reach your favorite spot? (This is a bit dramatic, but definitely an exercise in prioritizing what features you want to draw attention to with a pathway.)

Before You Begin

Map out your pathway before beginning a project. Sketch a diagram of your yard, and mark off areas such as planting beds, patios, water features, gardens, and other outdoor highlights. Now, with your answers to the questions above in mind, pencil in a line(s) to connect features. This line represents a potential pathway. Perhaps your goal is to establish a walkway from the back or front door of your home to an outdoor sitting area. Maybe you want a path to guide you through a garden, or a trail, so children can go from the back door to a swing set.

Did you place the line in the right place? Now is the time to play around with options and answer any what-if questions before digging out turf.

Next, walk the path you diagrammed, and take note of your stride. How much space do you need between each stepping stone? While walking the proposed pathway, sprinkle some household flour on each footstep. This will provide a rough placement guide for stepping stones.

Test out placement by cutting out cardboard pieces in the shape of the stones you will use. Create circles, squares, or misshapen pieces—just be sure that they are sized to match the stepping stones you plan to purchase. (This exercise is appropriate for installing a stepping stone pathway, not an interlocking brick or paver walkway, such as those pictured in the Design Inspiration section on page 135.) You can lay out the actual stepping stones, but you may find that you need to purchase more to complete your path. Making extra trips to the store adds unnecessary time to this project. Using cardboard cutouts before purchasing materials ensures that you procure all the supplies you need at once.

Materials Matters

From the variety of materials available today, you can choose stone that highlights Roman statuary, complements existing hardscapes, such as retaining walls, or meshes seamlessly with nature. Choose the most practical material for the shape of your path and style of your landscape. Explore available options for materials—there are so many!

Bluestone: This blue-gray natural stone is a mixture of sand compound and quartz particles. Its color blends well into landscapes as a subtle, sophisticated finish. Available in many shapes and sizes, bluestone is sometimes called slate, because it is flat. This quality makes the slabs easy to install.

Flagstone: Flagstone is available in a number of quarried stones, including limestone, sandstone, slate, and shale. Cut into slabs of varying shapes, flagstone can be pieced together like a puzzle. Larger slabs are ideal

---

DESIGN TIP

Choose a natural stone that suits the style of your landscape. Learn what stones are indigenous to your area. You may find that these are cost-effective and readily available. What's more, the material will blend in with the environment.

You can install concrete and brick-paver walkways without using mortar. Simply pour a layer of sand over the desired area, and set pavers into the loose "grout." Sand is also a great foundation to use when you want the flexibility of rearranging the pavers in the walkway.

for stepping-stone paths. The finish of these quarried surfaces lends a natural look to a landscape.

Stepping Stones: Available in squares, circles, paint-blob shapes, and decorative molded styles, the precast concrete stepping stones sold at garden stores cater to traditional homeowners, as well as whimsical gardeners. You can even purchase kits to create your own stepping stones at home.

Concrete Pavers: You'll find pavers in various shapes, sizes, and finishes.

Brick Pavers: These resemble clay bricks but are available in a variety of colors and shapes with decorative edges. Brick pavers interlock and can even be used in driveways, so rest assured, they bear foot traffic. Pavers also serve as desirable patio surfaces.

Clay Bricks: Traditional kiln-fired bricks offer an Old World feel, especially if you collect artifact bricks with unusual characteristics, such as the stamped name of an old bricking company. Clay bricks make interesting accent paths in garden spaces.

Gravel: Keep it simple, by clearing a strip and pouring a gravel or pebble walkway. This material is often used in Zen-inspired spaces and around beds with drought-tolerant landscape plants, such as cactus. Pebble walkways also complement areas that feature prominent rocks as accent pieces.

Mulch: Spreading this groundcover material in an edged pathway provides a solution for woodsy environments.

Step-by-Step Pathway

THE SUPPLIES
- **Spade**
- **Rake**
- **Sand or compactable gravel**
- **Stepping stones**

THE STEPS

1. Place the stones in desired pathway (after testing options using cardboard cutouts). You haven't committed to the location yet—just arrange stones into a desired position.

QUICK TIP

When laying stepping stones, be sure to set them on a bed of gravel or sand, to provide proper drainage. Otherwise, your walkway could sink and shift, as pavers settle into the soil. They can also slide out of position if saturated soil carries pavers away from their designated spots.

2. Allow the stepping stones to rest in place for several days, to kill the grass underneath. This provides an outline for excavation and makes turf removal much easier.

3. Using a spade, dig around the outline of each stepping stone and excavate the area. Refer to the stone width as your guide. You want the stones to be flush with the ground once installed. To allow room for layer of sand, which stabilizes the stepping stone, dig each hole 2 inches (5.1 cm) deeper than the height of the stones. Spread sand in each hole.

4. Place stones in sand-filled holes. Sand serves as grout, filling in the small gaps between the hole and the surrounding turf. Add or remove sand until each stepping stone is secure.

OLD WORLD BRICK WALKWAYS can complement a home such as this one. The variety of hardscapes—brick with a fieldstone border—creates layers of texture in this landscape.

THESE CHUNKY CONCRETE PAVER SLABS connect a gazebo with an outdoor living room setting to a wooded area of this property.

MIX MEDIA by combining two types of pathway materials, such as pebbles and stepping stones. By using pebbles, this homeowner created a wide path, and the flat, rounded rock slabs add interest.

THIS FLAGSTONE WALKWAY paves the way through a stunning show of color. The variously shaped stones are arranged like puzzle pieces, and the surface complements the landscape's cottage feel.

Build a Pond

Water enchants. Its bubbling sound washes away tension, and its looking-glass surface invites us to stop, reflect, and relax. It's no wonder we spend vacations flocking to beaches, lakefronts, riverfronts—anyplace where water meets land. Water's meditative symphony has a lulling effect. In a landscape, water serves as a focal point—a backyard oasis—and ponds allow us to enjoy a mental getaway on a smaller scale. Build one in a weekend, and enjoy it year-round.

Ponds are a serene centerpiece in a landscape. They transform a basic backyard landscape design into something striking and special—ponds pump up the wow factor. By adding water, you also broaden your plant palette. Aqua-loving plants add interest to garden-variety

Be sure to check for buried cables before you dig. Most communities offer a free "Dial before You Dig" service, in which someone marks your property for electrical, cable, gas, phone, and all other lines. Not sure how to locate this service? Call your utility company and ask for a recommendation.

landscapes, and the ecological benefits that ponds lend to your space make this project an aesthetic and sustainable venture.

Even better news: installing such a high-impact feature is not a lot of work. Materials are available to ease the process, and you can feasibly build an attractive, ecologically beneficial pond in an afternoon. Materials also cater to every price point, so don't let a pond's exotic look fool you into thinking that the project carries a hefty price tag. Garden stores, retail outlets, and companies that specialize in pond products stock an array of pond liners, pumps, and materials to make the job easy. You can also purchase kits—a convenient option.

Before You Begin

Don't dig into a pond installation project without considering the most important question: *where will you put it*? Placement of your pond is critical and, unfortunately, is often an afterthought for some homeowners. Don't assume that a focal point must be placed in the middle of the yard, and know that not just any clear space is suitable for a water feature. To position your pond to stay clean and healthy, consider all the placement obstacles in your backyard.

- **Where are trees located?** Do roots protrude?
- **What areas are exposed** to direct sunlight, and for how long?
- **Is your property on a slope?** Is there a level area in your yard?
- **Where do you like to relax outdoors?** Do you want to view the pond from a patio, or would you like to create a separate "room" in your backyard, with seating and plant life around the pond?

Most aquatic plants need four to six hours of direct sunlight, and mature tree canopies can block rays for most of the day in some cases. Keep this in mind. Examine your backyard for shade and sun, and note spaces that offer a combination of both.

Avoid treed areas. Protruding tree roots can prevent you from digging a pond—or you may run into them later in the installation process, if you're building a particularly deep pond. You can risk damaging the tree if you disturb the roots. Also, a pond placed directly under a tree will collect leaves and other debris, which means you'll be cleaning it often.

As you're observing your property's sun/shade pattern, also note its grade. You obviously do not want to install a pond on a slope, unless you plan to build up the grade, and that process requires a great deal of work and assistance from a professional.

When positioning your pond, be sure you have access to electricity and water. Pumps and filters require power, and you'll want to replenish the water supply in your pond regularly, especially during hot, dry weather.

Ponds range in shape and size, so unleash your creativity—imagine the design possibilities. Perfect circles and elegant ovals are traditional, but amoeba-shaped ponds are just as easy to accomplish. Build a Japanese garden around a rectangular pond that resembles an Old World reflecting pool. Tuck a water feature into a backyard corner, to which you can escape with a book and lounge in a favorite chair. Often, homeowners choose to use the pond as an anchor feature and design landscape and living spaces around it.

WATER ADDS movement and energy to a landscape.

Finally, note where you spend your time outdoors. You want to enjoy the pond, so place it in a location that is visible from a patio or seating area. Consider ways to position the feature so you can take advantage of its aesthetic appeal year-round. Do you want to see the pond from indoors? Water features add interest to a living room, if you can see the pond through a window.

After considering your property's characteristics and your goals for the pond, draw a map of your property. This working diagram should include relevant features, such as decks, patios, trees, flower beds, and gardens. Shade in areas that receive inadequate sunlight, and mark areas in which the grade or obstructions such as tree roots will make installation difficult. Treat this diagram as a map, and pick a plot for your pond. Later, you can refer to your drawing during the installation process.

Step-by-Step Pond
THE SUPPLIES
- **Pond liner**
- **Garden hose**
- **Spade**
- **Shovel**
- **A straight piece of lumber**
- **Carpenter's level**
- **Concrete blocks or stones** (to secure lining on edges)
- **Flagstone or decorative edging of your choice**

THE STEPS

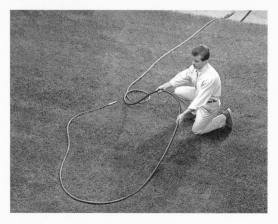

1. Select a site for your pond that is based on your property diagram, considering shade/sun and obstacles. Use a garden hose to outline the

pond shape. A hose is a flexible tool for marking off the area to excavate; you can adjust it into smooth, natural curves. Take your time and play with various shapes and arrangements, referring to your diagram, if necessary. Step back from the shape you create and be sure it complements the surroundings.

2. Position a garden spade or shovel at an angle and dig into the ground just outside of the hose outline. Remove dirt, excavating the pond area to a depth of about 10 to 12 inches (25.4 to 30.5 cm). This is the depth of the pond shelf. (Your pond will have levels when it is finished: rim, shelf, and bottom.)

3. Next, excavate the center of the pond to its maximum depth—18 to 24 inches (45.7 to 61 cm)—digging 2 inches (5 cm) deeper, to allow room for a layer of sand.

Note: Be sure to remove debris and rocks from the pond floor. You can use a two-by-four or tamper to pack down the bottom and create a smooth finish, so the liner will lay flat.

6. Size the pond liner to fit the excavated area. To determine the size, draw an imaginary square around the pond perimeter. You can mark this square with sand or baking flour if you wish, but this is not necessary. Measure the length and width of the square. Then, multiply the pond's maximum depth by two, and add three feet for the shelf and extra room for the liner to settle. The sum of these measurements is the size you should cut your liner.

4. Once you dig out the pond area, place a straight piece of lumber across the pond to check that the rim is level. Use a carpenter's level for accuracy. (Place the level on top of the lumber strip.) Remove or add dirt in high or low spots, until the pond is even across the top.

5. You'll want to add a border around your pond, to mask the pond liner and neaten the pond edge. Dig a shallow bed around the perimeter of the pond, just wide enough to accommodate flagstone or another type of border.

DESIGN TIP

Flexible pond liners come in a variety of materials, including polyethylene, polyvinyl chloride (PVC), and synthetic rubber sheeting. Polyethylene tears and cracks easily. Mid-priced PVC is more durable but does not last as long as synthetic rubber. You can count on rubber liners to stand up to sunlight, frost, and ice pressure. Also, this material is safe for plants and fish. While rubber liners are a bit more expensive, the availability of pond kits today makes the project affordable, no matter what material you choose. Also, the ease and convenience of pond kits is a plus for amateur landscapers. (That applies to most of us!)

8. Place some stones around the perimeter of the pond to hold down the liner.

9. Gradually fill the pond, smoothing out any wrinkles in the liner as the water level rises. Once the pond is full, remove the stones and allow time for the liner to settle.

10. Trim the liner, so that it forms a 4- to 6-inch (10.2-cm to 15.2-cm) border around the perimeter of the pond. You may wish to use galvanized spikes to fix it in place. Finish the pond by laying a border of flagstone, bluestone, or concrete pavers on the shallow bed you dug around the perimeter. Build up several layers of stone, for a raised look, or use a single layer, so the pond is level with the ground.

7. Spread a 2-inch (5.1 cm) layer of sand on the pond bottom and shelf, so the liner will lay on a smooth surface. Then, carefully place the liner into the pond bed by positioning it over the hole and slowly lowering it into place until it drops to the bottom. Ask your family or a friend to help you with this. The liner is much easier to handle with a couple of extra hands.

DESIGN TIP

Avoid wrestling with stiff pond liner by allowing it to warm in the sun for a half-hour before setting it into the excavated area. The rubber material will become malleable and settle more smoothly into the pond floor and shelf.

Grow Your Own Cleaning Crew

A pond acts much like a humidifier, restoring moisture to the atmosphere and creating a rich microclimate for plant life. Building a water feature into your landscape expands your planting options to include aqua-loving varieties such as water lilies, irises, ornamental grasses, and water hyacinths. With water-garden plants, you can create a diverse ecosystem in your backyard and maintain a clean, healthy pond.

Water-garden plants are beneficial for a number of reasons. Mainly, they restore oxygen to the pond and help establish an ecological balance in your backyard water community. If a pristine, clear pond is your goal, consider growing some "helpers," to keep the environment clean. You might think that plants will clutter your pond—make it look dirty, or invite in pests and insects. The opposite is true. Think of these plants as the clean-up crew. Algae won't compete with your water garden for nutrition. And shade from plant foliage can discourage algae growth.

There are various types of plants you can grow in or near water. Some stay submerged, others float, and you'll find various species that thrive in the shallow water near the edge of the pond. Incorporate a mix of plants, to preserve your pond's ecological balance: oxygenating plants (underwater plants that absorb nutrients and carbon dioxide); surface plants, such as water lilies, that provide shade; and bog plants that consume nitrogen and phosphates and also help to keep the pond

clean. You'll need to prepare pots for plants with submerged roots; you'll place these at the bottom of your pond.

Consider adding a couple of fish to your pond. They will feast on pests. Water snails munch on algae and nibble on decomposed plant material.

In addition to preserving your pond's ecological balance, plants also attract interesting wildlife. Your backyard becomes a show, when butterflies and birds play by the water feature. And, as construction in urban areas forces toads, frogs, and other small creatures from their natural habitat, your pond is a small step toward inviting them home. (This is not to say your backyard pond will be a breeding ground for them; rather, you are reducing the stress that modern environments inflict on nature's balance.) In essence, your pond is more than an eye-catching feature. It's a modest effort to restore habitat on your property.

THIS SMALL POND features a small show of aquatic plant life— enough to add interest and benefit the water quality.

✎ PREFORMED PONDS

AN ALTERNATIVE TO FLEXIBLE LINERS are preformed shells, which are made of plastic or fiberglass and are available in a variety of shapes, sizes, and textures. The downside to preformed ponds is that they can be cumbersome and difficult to transport. However, flexible granite forms are now available, and their rock finish is more natural than the stark black of most preformed shells. Also available are foldable liners, which are preshaped but not rigid, so they are easy to transport from the store to the pond site.

There are pros and cons to preformed pond liners, and, depending on your design goal, you may prefer to use the flexible liners we described in our steps on page 140. Preformed pond pros include guaranteed shape and depth, easy installation, and durability. But preformed ponds can cost more, are restricted to available shapes and designs, and look less natural in the landscape.

Regardless of which you choose, you'll enjoy the aesthetic qualities a pond lends to an outdoor space.

Prevent Pond Scum

Plants create a beneficial ecosystem in your pond, but their oxygenating powers are often insufficient to prevent stagnant water. When water lacks oxygen, it not only looks funky and full of scum (imagine a retention pond), the unappealing smell will drive you away from the feature you installed to enjoy. Small ponds are especially susceptible to algae/debris overload, because they are so contained. When nutrients from fertilizers, fish food, animal waste, soil, leaves, and rainwater enter the pond, they can build up into an algae problem.

MOVING WATER from this modest-sized waterfall helps oxygenate the pond.

Algae is just as vital as other plants to a pond's ecological balance, but, in excess, it deprives other organisms of oxygen. Essentially, the bad guys will suck all the nutrients from the good guys. The result—a stinky, green pond.

You can build a small pond without a pump or filter, but you are probably inviting water quality problems. To maintain oxygen levels in a pond, consider installing a small waterfall or spray jet—anything to keep the water moving. Or, play it safe and install a filtration system that will prevent your pond water from turning green.

There are two types of filtration systems: mechanical and biological. Some are two-in-one systems. Mechanical systems filter debris and algae, while biological filters oxygenate the pond, so beneficial bacteria will thrive. Biological filters are essential if your pond contains fish, because these systems break down pollutants and toxic ammonia from fish waste. Be careful not to clean biological filters, however—this will destroy their resident algae-fighting bacteria.

For small ponds without fish, mechanical filters are sufficient. You can purchase a submersible (internal) filter and set it into a pond, away from mud and plant material that will prevent it from doing its job. Be sure the discharge hose stays submerged at the bottom of the pond. You can also hook this hose to a fountain, waterfall, or other spraying feature. If you plan to add fish to your pond, install a

---

✎ DESIGN TIP

If you plan to grow aquatic plants, you'll need to make sure your pond is deep enough to accommodate them. Deep-water plants require at least 6 feet (1.8 m) of water to thrive, whereas shallow water plants are hardy in an average 1-foot (30.5-cm) water depth. Do your homework before digging the pond, so you don't limit your options. Talk to a local nursery and ask for tips from other water gardeners. You can find people who know their stuff through local garden clubs.

If your pond contains fish, remove them before adding more tap water to the pond. Allow the water to sit a few days, to dechlorinate. It is then safe to return the fish to the pond.

biological filter. A mechanical system alone will not convert harmful toxins.

You will need a pump to operate a filter, and you'll want to make sure this pump will handle your filter requirements. Your best bet is to talk to a pond professional. Check package labels, and, when choosing a pump, err on the side of more pump power.

Pond Maintenance

All ponds require maintenance to sustain their delicate ecological balance. By keeping up with basic tasks such as trimming plants and removing leaves, you can prevent algae buildup and other problems down the road. Following

are some pond clean-up tips to observe during seasons when the pond is in use.

- **Remove leaves and debris** from the pond surface.
- **Weed out invasive plants** and trim unruly ones; aim for 40 to 60 percent plant coverage.
- **Replenish pond water** during drought conditions, when levels run low.
- **Clean algae from pumps and filters.** Remember, do not clean out biological filters.
- **Control runoff,** by avoiding fertilizing areas that may drain into the pond—fertilizer runoff throws off the ecological balance of your pond and promotes algae growth.

A POND IS A BACKYARD OASIS for homeowners who treat the feature as the focal point of their landscape design.

Add Night Lights

Sunset doesn't have to dictate closing time for your outdoor living room. With the flip of a switch, you can show off that colorful plant bed you so carefully planted. Pay tribute to that favorite, old oak tree. Let's not forget the gurgling water feature you can hear, but not see, after dark. Set a sultry mood for dinner on the patio, and allow soft lights to tease some night moves from your favorite landscape features. Capture nature's nightlife with low-voltage lighting, and turn on your property's after-five appeal.

Landscape lighting extends the usability of outdoor spaces, and its benefits are threefold: aesthetics, value, and safety. Low-voltage lighting can accent your home's architectural character and highlight favorite landscape features. The showy result pumps up curb appeal, increasing your home's value. And lighting dark areas will discourage unwanted visitors from invading your privacy.

Most of all, lighting creates drama. The contrast between light and shadow introduces new shapes and angles at night and provides a different perspective from the daytime view. Lighting truly allows you to capitalize on your landscape investment, because you can enjoy outdoor features year-round, from the view of a window or while relaxing on your deck.

Installing low-voltage landscape lighting is safe and simple, thanks to today's prepackaged kits and widely available architectural-grade fixtures. But, before digging into an outdoor lighting project, set aside time to create a rough plan. Following are a couple of guidelines to consider.

Less is More: Add path lights gradually; step back to see whether your fixture arrangement illuminates dark spots. Don't place lights too closely together. Allow the beam to fill the space between each fixture. You don't want your property lit up like a ballpark, and your neighbors probably wouldn't appreciate that, either.

Layer Lights: Install the right fixtures in the right places. Choose spotlights for intense, specific uplighting and path lights to illuminate walkways and feature plants. To layer lighting, think in tiers: spotlight focal points, softly illuminate paths, and shine surface lights on porches or landings.

Before You Begin

Sketch a basic map of your property, drawing in plant beds, walkways, driveways, trees, shrubs, and other features. Ideally, you will plan lighting as you install other landscape features, but it's often an afterthought—one worth the afternoon it takes to install some simple fixtures. Creating a map is an important preinstallation step that will help you decide where to place fixtures. It will also help you determine how much wire and how many fixtures to purchase.

Low-voltage lighting is widely available in retail home stores, but you may want to consult a professional for design advice. Lighting is as much an artistic expression as the plants you choose for your landscape and the furniture you buy for your interior. Invest in an expert opinion if you feel overwhelmed by the possibilities.

Choose a few focal points you want to highlight. These might include a couple of interesting trees, a plant bed, a water feature, or a walkway you wish to illuminate for guests.

- **Note available outdoor** electrical outlets.
- **Mark dark spots** in corners or behind bushes and potentially hazardous steps and curbs.
- **Plot the placement** of outdoor lights. Eleven-watt bulbs cast 4 feet (1.2 m) of light, and path lights are generally available in 20 watts or less.

LIGHTING ARRANGED IN TIERS creates a natural effect—like moonlight. Your neighbors shouldn't feel like they live next door to a stadium. Choose a few focal points and, remember, less is more. You can add lights later if you find dim spots.

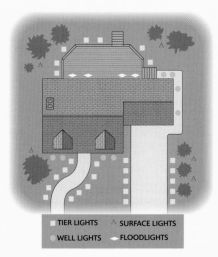

TIER LIGHTS   ∧ SURFACE LIGHTS
WELL LIGHTS   ◆ FLOODLIGHTS

Before you dig into a lighting project, sketch a rough plot of your property, identifying features such as trees, plant beds, and walkways. This will help you figure out areas to light.

Fixtures

Be sure that the fixtures you purchase are rated as water-resistant and are approved by the Underwriter's Laboratory (UL) for outdoor use. Never use interior lights outdoors. Also, if you plan to add lighting fixtures to a water feature, ensure that fixtures are labeled for this application.

Lighting sets and separate fixtures are available from retail home outlets and select garden stores. Kits generally include fixtures, a long wire, a controller (to turn lights off and on), and a transformer. Single fixtures, sold á la carte, are convenient for adding onto an existing lighting project or for illuminating a single feature. Also available are high-end, architectural-grade fixtures, which come in a variety of contemporary finishes, such as brushed copper. These luminaries are built to last, and you can expect them to light your landscape for ten to fifteen years. Prepackaged kits generally fizzle after a few years. With lighting, you get what you pay for.

Your choice of fixtures will depend on your experience and comfort level with low-voltage lighting, as well as your expectations for the results. Architectural-grade fixtures generally use halogen bulbs to cast a focused white beam, for a natural look. Lighting sets provide a quick and simple solution for homeowners who want to install path lighting. Both are easy to install, as long as you avoid common low-voltage traps (see page 152). When purchasing any fixture at a retail store, discuss your plans with an in-house specialist, to determine which product is the best fit for your project.

Path Lights

Path lights are available in styles and finishes to suit almost every taste. Mariners can find lighthouse fixtures; gardeners can buy fixtures that resemble flowers. Lantern-style fixtures are also popular. Tall bollard lights add height, shorter yard lights highlight low plants, and decorative lights in bronze, black, and diecast metal finishes can complement a landscape. If subtlety is your goal, veer toward conservative options. The fixture itself adds interest.

THIS PATH LIGHT is an affordable fixture you can find at most retail homes stores. Buy them in a set or individually. Avoid placing them too close together or installing too many of them in one place. A good rule of thumb is to place fixtures 10 feet (3 m) apart, though this measurement varies, depending on voltage output.

THESE FIXTURES ARE THE MOST COST-EFFECTIVE. Some homeowners install them as temporary light sources for outdoor parties.

Spotlights

Spotlights are versatile and highlight structural features. Hide them from view by planting groundcover or low-growing plantings nearby. Spotlights accent specific features, such as trees and sculpture. The beam is direct, and the fixture can be adjusted to accommodate the height of the desired feature.

Solar Lights

Solar lights, which use solar energy, instead of wiring, are a low-maintenance way to light a path—just don't expect the high-impact results you get from low-voltage lighting. The actual fixture looks no different than its cousin, the path light, but the beam from a solar light is not as intense. Because their voltage depends on how much sunlight the solar panels absorb during the day, you can't expect consistent light from these fixtures. However, their soft glow is appealing to homeowners who want a quick fix to light a path or low-growing plants.

Specialty Lights

A large assortment of decorative lighting options on the market provides practical and whimsical ways to add panache to a patio area. For function, mounted lights installed on deck posts illuminate eating and grilling areas. For fun, string nylon lantern lights around a patio or in low-hanging tree branches, to create a party atmosphere. Water lights add sparkle to ponds and fountains.

DESIGN TIP

Lighting professionals recommend mushroom-capped lights, rather than the pagoda-style path lights often sold in kits. Capped lights direct light downward and avoid the airport runway effect. Fixtures should not exceed 2 feet (61 cm) in height.

To conserve energy, consider installing a timer on your low-voltage system, so lights don't burn during daylight, or use Energy Star—labeled fixtures available with fluorescent and high-intensity bulbs. Lighting one 60-watt—equivalent porch light all night, every night, can cost next to nothing in electricity per year.

Design Techniques

Using landscape lighting in moderation, by incorporating a mix of fixtures and thoughtful placement, enhances your home's architecture, as well as the interesting plants and structural features in your outdoor living room. This project chapter will help you install path lights, but it's a good idea to understand how different light fixtures are used, so that if you decide to add on to your path-light project, you can do it with design savvy.

Uplighting

This is a dramatic way to light trees. Well lights are buried in the ground and shine up at branches. Above-ground directional lights are flexible and ideal for trees that aren't yet mature.

Downlighting

Mount lights on trellises, gazebos, mature trees, or the eaves of your home, to illuminate areas in which you eat, cook, or play.

Moonlighting

A full moon casts a white glow down through trees and over plants and the low-growing landscape. The dappled pattern moonlighting creates looks natural. You can achieve this effect by mounting lights in trees, pointing some of them down to cast light and draw out shadows from plantings. Lights pointed upward will highlight branches and foliage.

BY PLACING FIXTURES THAT SHINE up on trees, lighting designer Randall Whitehead transforms this property into a moonstruck portrait.

QUICK TIP

The maximum output wattage varies with the transformer model. If you exceed the transformer's maximum wattage, the lighting system will fail. Always check the wattage of light fixtures, do the math, and avoid overloading your transformer. (For example, a 100-watt transformer will accommodate up to nine 11-watt fixtures.) This is especially important if you are buying single fixtures or adding fixtures to an existing wire.

Backlighting

Backlighting washes light on walls, trellises, and fences, to create silhouettes of nearby trees and plantings.

Color Correcting

Many outdoor lights cast an amber glow, a warm, yellowish light that actually makes plants look sick. A silvery, blue light makes plant colors pop. Purchase daylight, blue, color-correcting filters for outdoor lights, and avoid using the red or yellow filters that come in some lighting kits. Unless you want your backyard to look like a carnival, consider saving these filters for holidays.

Step-by-Step Low-Voltage Lighting

THE SUPPLIES

- **Outdoor electrical cable** (one wire for each fixture)
- **Lighting fixtures**
- **Transformer**
- **Timer** (optional)
- **Shovel** for digging a shallow trench

THE STEPS

1. Connect the transformer to an outdoor electrical outlet. (Safety Warning: Follow directions on package to avoid electrical connection hazards.) The transformer converts electricity to the 12-volt level that outdoor lighting requires. It's generally a good idea to buy a transformer with more capacity than you need, so you have the option of adding fixtures later.

2. Measure the distance between your outdoor electrical outlet and the placement location of your last light. To prevent voltage drop, place your last fixture no farther than 75 feet (22.9 m) from the transformer. (See page 154.)

3. Lay out the fixtures and wire. Each fixture gets its own wire. Allow some slack in your cable (up to 5 feet [1.5 m] per fixture), so you can stagger fixtures along curves and adjust them if necessary. If installing lights near immature plants, you'll want to eventually move the fixtures out to accommodate growth. Bunch wires to form a neat cable to connect to your transformer.

4. Use a spade or small shovel to create a shallow trench along the bed in which you want to bury the cable. If you prefer, cut a 45-degree angle in the lawn surface, pry up the turf, and place the cable under the sod blanket. Don't get carried away—low-voltage cables can be buried just under the soil surface or be hidden with edging, mulch, or groundcover.

5. Place fixtures in desired locations. Place halogen path lights approximately every 10 feet (3 m), adjusting them according to how much light they put out. This guideline applies to 20-volt lights. Be sure your last path light is no farther than 75 feet (22.9 m) from the transformer, if you want consistent light.

6. Connect each end of the wire to the transformer taps, which look like small pegs located on the bottom of the transformer. (Again, read directions carefully on the transformer. It will guide you as to which tap to use for lights closer and further away.)

7. Set automatic timer, if you opt to install one.

DESIGN TIP

Use discretion with spotlights. Choose a couple of priority features to highlight, and apply shields to lights to avoid glare if they are visible.

If you do not know the location of underground wires and pipes, call your utility company and ask them to mark these spots before you dig.

Troubleshooting Voltage Drop

Wondering why the fixture farthest away is so dim? The reason is voltage drop, when power literally runs down by the time it reaches the last fixtures. Lighting kit usually supply only a single wire for all fixtures; the result is that lights farthest from the transformer get less power than the first one in line. To illuminate fixtures evenly and avoid voltage drop, be sure not to exceed 75 feet (22.9 m) in distance from the transformer. (If you stretch a fixture too far, it will be much dimmer than the rest. Not attractive.) If you use a kit, check the package for distance allowance.

One way to prevent voltage drop is to attach each fixture to a separate wire. Purchase a transformer with multiple taps, to which you can connect wires. These taps are designed to feed more power to far-away fixtures, distributing voltage evenly.

Q: What trends have you noticed in outdoor landscape lighting?

A: First, more people are creating outdoor rooms. They are investing in the equity of their homes and realizing they have all this space outside that has yet to be explored. So they design landscapes and areas in which they can entertain al fresco. They have spent a lot of money and time to create a wonderful outdoor environment, and they want to enjoy it when daytime falls into darkness.

One lighting technique that is growing popular is the moonlighting effect. Instead of ground-mounting all lighting, we are placing fixtures under the eaves of main buildings, inside trellises and pergolas, and on tall trees. These fixtures project light downward and create a dappled pattern of light and shadow. We see this effect during a full moon. People want to re-create that feel.

Q: When is the best time for homeowners to plan outdoor lighting?

A: Plan your lighting before, not after, the landscape is completed.

If you are going to spend the time and energy on landscaping, you should really think about how to light it as you plan the design. While you are digging trenches for irrigation systems or fountain pumps, it's a good time to lay wiring for landscape lighting.

Q: What is the most flexible, multipurpose fixture available?

A: A shielded directional light, which can be mounted under the eaves of buildings, inside gazebos, at the base of sculptures, and around fountains. It looks like a juice can with a stake in it. The light is in the bottom of the can, so there is less glare.

Hiring a Professional

Nothing is more satisfying than enjoying a patio you helped to build or clipping flowers from a garden that you established with your own hands. Landscape projects instill a sense of pride and accomplishment in homeowners who choose to take charge. But even green thumbs and handymen—do-it-yourself veterans—have weak points. A green thumb who loves gardening might

need help building a patio, and even if you work well with your hands, you might benefit from some planting advice.

Hiring a professional to assist with landscape projects or to manage maintenance can relieve the burden of keeping up your curb appeal and leave you free to engage in the projects you enjoy. Contract a lawn care service to worry about fertilizer and other weed-control applications, and manage the mowing yourself, if that is your outdoor therapy. The same philosophy applies to large-scale projects. Decide what you can realisti-

cally handle and when you would be better served hiring help. Time management is an issue for everyone, and, by delegating tasks you don't want to handle to professionals, you can reserve time for projects you *want* to do yourself.

As with any project, do your homework before hiring a professional. Following are some points to consider as you seek out the best person for the job.

Select Services

What type of services are you seeking? Experts in various aspects of landscape design, installation, and maintenance bring different strengths to the table.

Landscape Contractor: If you want someone to mow and edge your lawn and provide optional aeration and leaf-cleanup services in the fall, hire a landscape contractor. These service professionals specialize in maintenance.

Lawn-Care Professional: Fertilization and preemergence and postemergence lawn care applications can help you sustain a weed- and insect-free lawn. Lawn care technicians are trained in chemical applications, are equipped to do it efficiently and safely, and can diagnose disease and weed problems that you may not notice. If you enjoy performing weekly maintenance, do the mowing yourself, then hire a pro to manage your lawn-care program, so you can ensure that your property gets proper doses of essential nutrients.

Irrigation Technician: Irrigation work is technical and can be labor intensive. For complex, in-ground irrigation systems, a professional technician can design, install, and manage annual upkeep.

Landscape Architect: These professionals are schooled in landscape design and hold licenses. They are the creativity behind building projects—the idea people who can introduce possibilities. Often, landscape architects work within design/build firms. These companies are one-stop shops, providing design and installation services under one roof. This setup is convenient for homeowners who want a seamless transition from planning to execution.

Nursery Professionals: Garden centers are a wonderful resource for homeowners who are planting flower beds and gardens themselves. Garden-center nursery professionals can help you choose plant material.

Tree Care Specialists: Tree care requires special equipment and expertise. Often, the scope of a tree project is too great for a homeowner to manage.

(Consider those cranes they often need to trim tall trees.)Tree care professionals can remove stumps, prune and cut back large trees, and clean-up heavy, hanging branches and debris after a storm. For safety's sake, consider hiring a tree specialist, rather than taking on these potentially dangerous projects yourself.

Find the Best Fit

Now that you know which experts can help you care for your property, where will you find the best one for the job? Many professionals in the green industry rely on word-of-mouth advertising, so the best place to start is by talking with neighbors, friends, and colleagues. Which companies do they trust? Stop in at your local garden store and see if a staff member will recommend a list of service professionals. You should call more than one for an estimate. Another way to start is by contacting trade associations, such as the Professional Landcare Network (PLANET). As the voice of the green industry, this association can guide you to certified landscape contractors in your area.

Other important factors to consider when looking for a company to perform landscape services: licensing, certification, and insurance. Ask the following questions:

- **Do you belong** to a professional trade association? Which one?
- **Are you** licensed or certified?
- **Do you have** proof of insurance and bonding?
- **Can you show** me examples of your work? (Ask for photos or properties you can visit, to see end results)
- **What is** your specialty?

Call the Better Business Bureau to be sure the service you are considering engages in sound business practices. There are many fly-by-nighters out there—two-truck tag teams that aren't insured or licensed and certainly won't guarantee their work. If you want a job done well, check the company background, and be sure to hire someone with experience and training.

Price Matters

Pricing and fee schedules depend on the type of service you need. For maintenance and lawn care, you can pay per week, month, or season. Companies sometimes offer specials to customers who commit to a year-long contract, but you may prefer the flexibility of pay-as-you-go services. Design/build firms price services by project, and fee arrangements vary, depending on the provider.

Regardless of the type of service you require, you should set a budget before meeting with a professional. This is especially true for design/build services, which manage large-scale projects. Before your first meeting, determine how much you can or want to invest. Often, large projects are planned in phases, so you are billed in bite-sized chunks. Set limits, then discuss these with the landscape contractor, so neither party is disillusioned going into the project.

But wait—did you consult with several different service providers? If the answer is no, review your reference list, and call at least one more company for an estimate before you sign that contract. Due diligence is your responsibility. Get at least two itemized bids for your project, and ask for set start and finish dates. Review the pros and cons of your options, and *don't let price be the deciding factor*. As with anything, you will get from your project what you are willing to put into it. If you compromise quality materials or expert craftsmanship to spare a few bucks, you'll regret the nominal savings down the road, when you must hire someone new to replace plant material or rebuild flimsy construction.

The Contract

Entering a relationship with a landscape professional is like making any business agreement. Test the waters before assigning a significant amount of responsibility to a service provider with whom you've never worked. Phased installation projects are a great way to determine a company's commitment to quality, timeliness, and professionalism. For example, if your plan is to build an entire outdoor living room over the period of a few summers, start with the deck and hire a company for just this portion of the project. (Don't invite several different companies to work on various parts of your landscape at the same time—this displays a lack of professionalism on your part.) Don't contract for your whole backyard at once. Sign on for one phase and take it in steps, so that if you are dissatisfied with a company's service, you won't have to face the next season already contracted with them.

A word on honoring contracts: When you sign on the dotted line, you make a promise to the company to fulfill your duties as a customer. You confirm the scope of the project, materials, project timeframe, and fee schedule. If you have done your homework, your experience working with a professional will be a positive one.

Seasonal Maintenance Checklists

Plants have a biological clock, just as humans do. Mother Nature controls it by setting the temperature, but you are the one who can prepare your lawn and landscape to weather these seasonal changes. Your lawn lives and breathes, and it requires year-round care if you expect strong performance. Tending to turf's nutritional needs in the fall, so it can withstand a harsh winter, or preparing it in the spring for a summer of growth—how you treat your lawn one season will influence its luster the next.

This doesn't mean you need to labor outdoors every day to get the results you want. Just review the following checklists and keep up regular maintenance, so the chores don't build up on you.

Your lawn care responsibilities will vary according to whether you live in a cool or warm climate. Warm-season grasses grow and repair more quickly in summer; cool-season grasses repair in fall, when they aren't stressed by summer heat and dryness. Before beginning a project such as seeding, aeration, or planting, take into account when your turf undergoes the most stress. You want to perform these tasks when your lawn is best able to recover.

Refer to one of the following checklists that corresponds with your climate. Understand that transition zones require a hybrid care schedule of sorts. You'll want to base your seasonal maintenance on the type of turf you grow.

Cool Climates

Spring

- **Service lawn mower:** sharpen blades, change oil and filter, and general tune-up (if you did not do so during winter—the ideal time); all of these services can be performed by a professional equipment dealer
- **Plant annuals**
- **Clean up leaves** and other debris cluttering beds
- **Lay fresh mulch** in landscape beds, to discourage weed growth and help plant roots retain moisture

- **Seed bare spots** in your lawn, or overseed (if you did not perform these tasks in fall)
- **Prevent weeds** by applying a preemergent application (see Chapter 4 for specifics)
- **Spot-treat weeds** as needed
- **Apply slow-acting fertilizer** to promote green-up (refer to Chapter 4)

Summer

- **Adjust mower** to the proper height for your turf variety; raise height to alleviate summer stress in cool-season grasses
- **Water** lawn as needed

Fall

- **Cut back** plant branches after the first hard freeze
- **Dead-head** perennial flowers by pinching off expired blooms; this encourages new growth in spring
- **Aerate** your lawn (if necessary) in early fall
- **Topdress or overseed** your lawn following aeration (if necessary)
- **Seed bare patches** or new lawns in early fall to allow time for germination and root development before winter
- **Remove leaves** from your yard and plant beds
- **Apply fall fertilizer** (refer to Chapter 4 for specifics)

Winter

- **Take your mower** in for service before the spring rush (sharpen blades, general tune-up)
- **Conduct an inventory** of your tools: What are you missing, what needs to be replaced, which tools need sharpening or cleaning?
- **Trim back trees and shrubs** (now is the ideal time, though you can trim moderately year-round)

Fall/Winter

- **Service** lawn equipment
- **Lay fresh** mulch in beds
- **Mow lawn regularly** if it is not dormant (overseeded Bermudagrass will require mowing)
- **Water** growing (overseeded) lawns on a regular basis

Warm Climates

The equipment maintenance reminders outlined above also apply in warm climates, but because warm-season grasses love hot, southern weather, spring and summer are the best times to plant.

Spring/Summer

- **Plug, sprig, or sod** bare patches and new lawns
- **Fertilize** and follow a regular lawn care program, with pesticide applications as needed (Note: A professional will best advise you on these preventive and curative applications)
- **Water** as needed
- **Adjust mower height** to appropriate level based on your turfgrass variety; cut lawn when needed
- **Aerate** or dethatch (if necessary)
- **Topdress or overseed** following aeration/dethatching (if necessary)
- **Plant** annuals

Turfgrass Varieties

Bent Grass

Characteristics: Creeping bent grass forms a dense mat with shallow roots. The grass spreads by above-ground stolons. Slender, smooth leaf blades are ridged on the underside and bluish-green in color.

Season: Cool season. Zones 4 to 8. Adapts well to cool, humid climates. Likes full sun and tolerates light shade. The main use of bent grass in the south is on golf greens, where it can be carefully managed.

Care: Bent grass will tolerate low mowing, which is one reason you see it on golf greens. However, the variety is high-maintenance and is prone to fungus. It also requires constant attention to water management, soil preparation, air circulation, and shade. Let a golf course maintenance crew deal with bent grass—the variety requires quite a bit of work for a home lawn. Unless kept short, it can look messy.

Bermuda Grass

Characteristics: Drought-tolerant and resistant to pests and disease, Bermuda grass is a wise choice for regions with abbreviated winters or none at all. Its texture is soft and fine, and it provides a dense carpet of green that wears well.

Season: Warm season. Zones 6 to 10. Southern, tropical, subtropical, and coastal climates are ideal for Bermuda grass, which is commonly found on sports fields, parks, and golf courses. You'll find Bermuda grass in more than 100 countries.

Care: Proper fertilization and mowing practices are key for sustaining healthy Bermuda grass. Grass goes dormant and turns brown in winter if planted in cool climates. It can be planted from seeds or sprigs and requires mowing twice a week while it is actively growing. Those who don't mind a strenuous care schedule will enjoy its attractive appearance.

Buffalo Grass

Characteristics: As its name suggests, buffalo grass once supported roaming herds of buffalo in the Great Plains. It is a true native—a survivor. It tolerates extreme temperatures and produces seed quickly. The grass spreads by stolons and seed and forms a fine-textured, thin turf with a blue-green color. It does not have underground stems. This grass is ideal for homeowners who want a native, low-maintenance landscape.

Season: Warm season. Zones 4 to 8. Dry summers and cold winters are fine for buffalo grass, but it does not respond well to humidity. The grass goes dormant from September to May.

Care: Mow buffalo grass just a few times each year—it will grow no higher than 5 inches (12.7 cm). Once established, the grass requires light watering and little fertilization. It's best for low-maintenance grounds and homeowners who want a native grass that provides a lawnlike appearance. Mow at 2 to 4 inches (5.1 to 10.2 cm).

Kentucky Bluegrass

Characteristics: If there is a portrait of a typical lawn, it probably contains Kentucky bluegrass. The most widely planted turfgrass type, it is often used in blends with perennial ryegrass or creeping red fescue to produce a more shade-tolerant, tough-wearing lawn. Kentucky bluegrass lawns are fine-textured and vigorous. The grass is named for its blue-green color.

Season: Cool season. Zones 2 to 7. Loves full sun, but certain blends will tolerate shade. The grass tolerates cold, survives drought by going dormant, and can generally withstand unforgiving environmental conditions.

Care: Kentucky bluegrass must be watered frequently, especially if you do not want your lawn to go dormant during a drought. Seeds are slow to germinate, and though you can purchase sod, it tends to be expensive. Mow at 1½ to 3 inches (3.8 to 7.6 cm).

Perennial Ryegrass

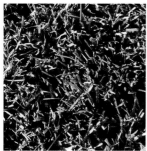

Characteristics: Common perennial ryegrass is an ideal filler. It germinates quickly, but because it grows in bunches, rather than spreading, perennial ryegrass is often mixed with other species. For example, perennial ryegrass paired with Kentucky bluegrass works well, because the ryegrass germinates rapidly and is wear-tolerant, while the Kentucky bluegrass's spreading habit repairs turf damage.

Another type of ryegrass, annual ryegrass, lasts for a 12-month period. This variety also germinates quickly, which makes annual ryegrass an ideal starter grass for new construction. Overseeding a brand-new lawn with annual ryegrass will ensure color and erosion protection while the main grass grows in.

Season: Cool season. Zones 3 to 7. Perennial ryegrass likes full sun and will tolerate minimal shade. It thrives in cool, moist areas with mild winters.

Care: Perennial ryegrass tolerates heavy foot traffic; its wear tolerance is better than most cool-season grasses. You'll want to water perennial ryegrass frequently, but it can survive drought periods. The grass is fairly low maintenance and should be mowed at 1½ to 2½ inches (3.8 to 6.4 cm).

St. Augustine Grass

Characteristics: The most popular lawn in the southern states, St. Augustine grass thrives in heat but does not perform in cool climates. It can stand moderate to heavy foot traffic and resists weeds. The grass is dense and attractive, though it will turn brown in winter.

Season: Warm season. Zones 8 to 10. Thrives in southern United States, along the Gulf Coast, in southern California, and in similar coastal/subtropical environments, because it can take salt spray and heat.

Care: St. Augustine grass tolerates full shade and loves sun. Water St. Augustine grass frequently. Beware of fungus and insects. Otherwise, the grass is fairly low maintenance and should be mowed at 2½ to 4 inches (6.4 to 10.2 cm).

Turf-Type Tall Fescue

Characteristics: A coarsely textured, rich-green grass, this variety differs from tall fescues and fine fescues, which have slender blades. It is quickly becoming a choice for home lawns and commercial sites because of its wear tolerance and resistance to drought and weeds. It has an extensive root system and spreads by bunch growth.

Season: Cool season. Zones 2 to 7. Adapts well to mild winters and warm summers.

Care: Overseeding every other year is sometimes recommended to improve the density; the thicker the turf stand, the thinner and more attractive the grass. Water infrequently and deeply. Mow this turf at 2 to 4 inches (5.1 to 10.2 cm).

Zoysia Grass

Characteristics: Coarse, needlelike blades make Zoysia grass wear tolerant, and its deep root system allows it to survive in drought conditions. Its leaf blades roll under, and it conserves moisture effectively, while at the same time responding to irrigation and rainfall. Zoysia bounces back. But it grows slowly and tends to go dormant in the cold sooner than other species.

Season: Warm season. Zones 6 to 9. Thrives in southern coastal areas and environments such as those of southern California. Sun-loving Zoysia grass tolerates shade, as well.

Care: Zoysia grass requires little water and does not perform well in soils with poor drainage. The grass is resistant to pests and disease. However, it spreads slowly and tends to need dethatching. Mow at 1¼ to 3 inches (3.2 to 7.6 cm).

Critter Control

Wildlife can destroy your carefully planted landscape, and it can protect your property by eating and scaring off detrimental insects. Nature provides us with natural pest controllers, such as birds, lizards, snakes, and bats. They eat for breakfast the same insects we might pay a service to exterminate.

Then there are the critters that wreak havoc.

You might like to watch deer prance through your snowy backyard—a perfect winter scene. But that animal is hungry, foraging for dinner. Virtually any plant in your lawn looks like gourmet grub, and once deer discover that your landscape is a lush salad bowl, they'll be back for more. Rodents and rabbits also like to gnaw on branches and plant material, and moles are underground excavators that will tear up your lawn. Even your own house pets can "overfertilize" your property and dig up sod.

The good news: You can attract the beneficial wildlife and discourage detrimental critters from stripping away and digesting your hard work. Some solutions include repellent sprays, netting to cover trees and shrubs, and reducing the number of appetizing insects that attract unwanted grazers through an Integrated Pest Management (IPM) program. Employing IPM controls pests in a safe, effective, long-lasting way and includes encouraging beneficial insects, growing pest-resistant plants, trees, and shrubs, and using selective pesticides.

But what if the damage is already done? How do you know which creature is the culprit? You can identify which critters are gnawing on plant life by their teeth marks.

Deer: Twigs and stems show a rough, shredded surface because deer lack upper incisors; deer also strip bark and leave no teeth marks

Rabbits: Neat, sharp 45-degree cuts

Rodents: Narrow teeth marks

Following are some typical habits you can expect from unwanted animal guests, as well as ways to prevent them from damaging plants and turf.

Deer

Deer are overpopulated in many suburban communities and driven to feed on landscaping, rather than native plants. In rapidly developing regions, deer seem to outnumber people. They're everywhere—mostly because we've moved into land that was once a buffet for animals, ripe with vegetation to chomp on. Just try to convince deer that your plant bed isn't as tasty. They aren't easily controlled.

Discouraging deer from feeding on your property is challenging, at best. If you use one type of repellent, they soon grow immune to the scent and return to munch on your shrubs. Maybe you've tried remedies such as leaving bars of soap in your lawn. They get used to this, too. There are plenty of products on the market designed to protect your landscape from their binges, but redirecting deer to a feeding area other than your yard is a task. The fact is, there is really no such thing as a deer-proof plant. If they're hungry enough, they'll snack on any variety available.

However, there are a few ways to minimize deer exposure. You can place netting over young shrubs and seedlings, and you can protect trunks with tubing. Fences can also keep deer off your property.

Following are some more specific instructions for controlling deer. (And if you have any other ideas, by all means, share!)

Netting and Tubing

Place netting around seedlings and small trees. Tubes protect tree trunks and young branches, although not all tubing will prevent bucks from scraping their antlers against tree trunks. You can also purchase paper bud caps, which form a protective cylinder around young plants, to reduce damage.

Fencing

A keep-out policy is only possible with fencing. There are several types: electric; a conventional 8-foot (2.4-m) fence of woven wire; single-wire electric fences; slanting fences; and mesh barriers. New products are regularly introduced into the market, and your choice will probably depend largely on how much you want to invest. Also, if your neighborhood or city has zoning regulations, a woven wire fence may not be possible for you.

Electrical fences may seem a harsh way to protect your landscape, but deer actually respond well to safe correction. They learn that plants beyond the barrier are not for them. If the deer population is low in your area, a single-wire electric fence will protect a plant-ing area. You can always add wires if the deer problem escalates. Deer will try to go under or through a fence, rather than over it, so for a double-wire fence, place wires at approximately 15 and 30 inches (38.1 and 76.2 cm) from the ground; in triple-wire electric fences, place them 10, 20 and 30 inches (25.4, 50.8 and 76.2 cm) from the ground. A two-dimensional fence design is also available. This is a fence within a fence, which provides a couple of layers of protection.

Repellents

Contact repellents are applied directly to plants and discourage deer foraging by creating a foul taste. Area repellents cover a problem area and control deer by emitting a bad smell.

A homemade remedy you can try is a spray consisting of 20 percent raw eggs and 80 percent water. This will last about 30 days and is weather resistant. Soap bars and human hair are also used to keep deer away from plants and trees, but neither of these methods has been proven effective. Even if they work for a short time, deer soon learn that the soap won't keep them from dinner.

Rodents

The word "rodent" sparks an immediate reaction of distaste in most homeowners—Yuck. The two most common rodents that can truly damage your lawn are moles and gophers. Both are stubborn, and they are difficult to tame, remove, and discern from one another. However, their features are quite different. Gophers snack on roots and plants, while moles like insects and worms. To accommodate their diets, gophers' teeth are equipped for tearing into plant material, while moles have snouts meant for digging. Tunneling and burrowing rodents such as gophers and moles leave their tracks in the form of disrupted turf and half-eaten garden vegetables.

Both rodents travel underground, so if your neighbors have a mole problem, or you notice telling crisscross mounds in their yards, you had better take measures to prevent the pests from crossing borders into your lawn. Following are some tips for preventing damage from these common rodents.

Moles

Moles are the size of chipmunks and like to burrow under the soil surface. Their powerful paws are digging and packing tools, helping them to create tunnels. As they build their underground highways, they push dirt to the surface. You'll notice their tracks in gardens and fresh turf; they appear as cracks in the soil—long veins. They can disrupt sidewalks, concrete, and even foundations. They are expert miners, and their tracks are much more visible than those of gophers.

But you don't have to see mole tunnels for evidence that they are burrowing under your lawn. If you find your feet sinking into a spot in your yard, or notice spongy areas in your turf, you could be trampling on a mole tunnel. You probably won't see their damage in the winter. They tend to hibernate in extreme cold, when they dig deeper into the ground and hide out until the weather breaks.

Mole Food
- **Grubs**
- **Insect larvae**
- **Worms**

Mole Control

Flooding and trapping will discourage mole invasion, the latter being a more effective method. To flood, run a garden hose through the hill, which is the entrance to the tunnel. The water will either scare the mole out of the hole or drown it. Be prepared to remove the mole once it surfaces.

Trapping moles in the spring or fall is really the best way to remove them. In the winter, they burrow down deep and hibernate, so they are difficult to locate. Set mole traps on surface feeder runs. Identify main runways by looking for tunnels that reopen and follow a fairly straight line, appearing to connect two mounds or feeding areas. These often align with fencing, walkways, and foundations.

There are several types of traps:
- **Harpoon**
- **Scissor-jaw**
- **Choker-loop**

All of these are effective. Be sure to read directions before setting the traps.

Ultimately, you can prevent moles by controlling grubs in your yard. If your soil has grubs, chances are great that moles are burrowing under your property, too. Consult a lawn care service to discuss grub prevention and treatment applications.

Gophers

Gophers are vegetarians, and these burrowing, foraging creatures can damage lawns considerably. Grass roots get a double hit: Gophers eat the roots, and water from sprinklers can run into gopher holes before getting a chance to saturate the soil and reach the root zone. Gophers tunnel deep under the surface—you'll rarely see them. You will notice their mounds, but don't expect to trap or poison them there. They live in their underground network, so control measures must focus on reaching their subsurface labyrinths.

Gopher Food
- **Plants**
- **Grass roots**
- **Garden vegetables**

Gopher Control

Stubborn and difficult to manage, gophers are a nightmare for gardeners and a frustration for homeowners who have ever tried to trap, poison, or gas them out of their holes. Think Bill Murray in the movie *Caddyshack*. Even scare tactics using dynamite don't work. Vibrating and ultrasonic devices are no more likely to budge gophers from their burrows than the humming sound your mower makes when you pass over their tunnels. There are plenty of homemade and unconventional remedies for removing gophers, too: road flares, human hair, you name it—none of them effective. So, don't bother stuffing things down the gopher hole.

Flooding doesn't work either, because gophers are skilled swimmers. If water gets too deep, they'll plug the tunnel.

Trapping, poison, and gasses are common control methods. Box traps are probably your best bet. Find the main tunnel, which is up to 12 inches (30.5 cm) below the surface. Stick a gopher probe into the mound and determine the direction of the tunnel. Dig two holes along the tunnel and set the traps, positioning their openings in opposite directions.

If you choose to use poison, avoid those containing strychnine—you might inadvertently poison your house pets or other animals that prey on rodents poisoned with this substance. Choose baits laced with anticoagulants, which are purported to kill gophers painlessly. You can purchase poison in grains or cakes. To use it, poke a metal rod or pipe into the burrow, then spoon the bait into the hole. Cakes require a larger hole and must be broken up carefully. While some report success by fumigating tunnels with gas, propane, or auto exhaust, this dangerous practice is *not* recommended. Why risk your own safety to get rid of a gopher? Think about it.

Squirrels

Squirrels are a nuisance, and they have a habit of hiding food in the small holes they dig in your plant and flower beds. Or, they are busy looking for food—still digging.

You can't eliminate squirrels, but you can stop tempting them with loosely thrown birdseed. Ask your neighbors to do the same. You can also discourage them from entering your home, by securing screen doors and windows. If your garage or screened porch serves as a nesting place for squirrels, you can expect to host their offspring, come spring.

Skunks

Got grubs? If so, your lawn is a feast not only for moles but skunks, too. Skunks love insects and larvae, and their nocturnal night hunts for these pests can result in peeled-up sod as they dig around for bug snacks. Their odorous reply to control tactics is quite unpleasant. Your best bet is to call your local animal game warden, who will investigate the situation and set live traps.

If a skunk sprays you or a house pet, acidic products such as vinegar and tomato juice will take the edge off the smell. But they won't alleviate the odor entirely. You can also purchase shampoos formulated to remove the smell.

House Pets

If the family dog has the run of the yard, you probably understand what nitrogen does to a lawn—your dog's "business" is the equivalent of superpowered fertilizer. When you pour pure fertilizer on your grass, you burn the lawn. The same chemistry applies to dog urine. And if your animal is a male, your bushes and plant beds will suffer, as well.

House pets also create other lawn and landscape hazards. Your dog might be a digger. Puppies can chew on sprinkler heads, fences, and many other objects in your yard. And as for the other half of pets' bathroom habits—the kind you step in and track into the house if you're not careful—well, this also contains nitrogen and can burn lawns (although feces works more like slow-release fertilizer, because the nitrogen breaks down gradually, leaving grass burns in its wake). Obviously, you don't want to run your mower over any of these surprises.

In addition to performing regular clean-up, one way to contain the damage caused by loving house pets is to give them a dedicated space for doggy business. (Side yards or areas that are less visible or prone to less foot traffic are the best places.) Train your animal to use this space exclusively. Your dog will learn this by scent. (Have you ever noticed that dogs like to go in places that other dogs have already marked?)

Sharing Space

A growing number of homeowners want to spend their free time in their own backyard and have designed their landscapes to serve as outdoor living rooms. Decks, fireplaces, comfortable furniture, showy plant beds, water features—the only thing missing is a pool bar. And a Members Only pass. The caveat to outdoor enjoyment is that you share the space with pests. Controlling the bad ones and inviting the good ones to be on your "team" is the best way to strike a balance. And, even as you train your pets and work to keep out burrowing rodents and hungry deer, remember there are interesting birds and beautiful bugs, such as butterflies, that you might want to attract. Talk to your garden center specialist about the native plant varieties that will welcome such wildlife. After all, what is more relaxing than putting up your feet and watching a show?

Resources

American Lawns
www.american-lawns.com

Colorado State Cooperative Extension
www.ext.colostate.edu

Dow Agrosciences
www.dowagro.com
(317) 337-3000

Hunter Industries
www.hunterindustries.com
USA headquarters: (760) 744-5240
Europe (France): (33) 4-42-37-16-90

John Deere
www.johndeere.com
Customer Contact Center: (800) 537-8233

Know Before You Mow
www.knowbeforeyoumow.org

North Carolina State University
North Carolina Cooperative Extension
www.ces.ncsu.edu/index.php?page=lawngarden

Penn State Center for Turfgrass Science
http://turf.cas.psu.edu/

Professional Landcare Network (PLANET)
www.landcarenetwork.org
(800) 395-2522

Texas A&M Turfgrass Program
AggieTurf Turf Answers 4 You
http://aggieturf.tamu.edu/./answers4you/index.htm

The Irrigation Association
www.irrigation.org
(703) 536-7080

The Ohio State University Extension
http://extension.osu.edu/index.php
(614) 292-6181

Acknowledgments

My sincere appreciation to Bill Klutho, for a surprising phone call introducing the opportunity to write this book. Thanks to the John Deere team, particularly Dean Hamke, the go-to guy; Mark Schmidt, for your poetic agronomics and careful eye; and Mike Ballou, for answering my mower questions over the phone, while actually mowing your lawn. That's dedication.

Thanks also to Jennifer Cox, Greg Weekes, Stephanie Boozer for their keen attention to detail and Mike Scaletta and Sean Overington for their design sensability. A collection of turfgrass professionals offered insight on their best practices (and bloopers)—information cultivated through years in the field, education, and plenty of research trials. Thank you Casey Reynolds, of North Carolina State University; Dave Gardner, of The Ohio State University Extension; Randall Whitehead of Randall Whitehead Lighting; Jamie Breuninger, from Dow Agrosciences; Rick Miralia, of Gale's Garden Center, Westlake, Ohio; and Bill Fields, from Lowe's Home Improvement.

An education as a *Lawn & Landscape* magazine staff member, along with a full bill of trade shows for several years, served as my foundation—call it Lawn U. This base has evolved into numerous creative adventures, for which I am thankful.

Most of all, thanks to Mom and Dad. You inspire, support, and understand. I still follow your recommendation to "Go play outside."

Thank you to a creative and enormously talented team at Quarry Books. Betsy Gammons, I'm so grateful that you allowed me to use your phone number as a support and help line! (I called it often!) David Martinell, John Hall, and Rosalind Wanke; the visual appeal of this book is thanks to your expertise. Thank you for asking the tough questions, and always having the answers.

And to Haven Ohly, my husband and best friend—a listener and kind soul. I learned the day after I finished this book that your name means "garden" in Norwegian. "Meant to be," my relative told me. I think so, too.

About the Author

Kristen Hampshire is an award-winning writer, whose work has been published in a wide variety of nationally recognized magazines. She served as editor for two green-industry publications, *Commercial Dealer* and Bayer Environmental Science's *Lawn Care Professional*. A curious mind draws Hampshire into a diversity of topics, from corporate profiles to travel and arts. Her specialty in style, design, and the way in which these elements merge in the landscape are subjects she covers regularly for newspapers and a range of landscape- and interior-focused publications. A foundation in lawn and landscape knowledge gained from trade journals serves as a base for practical, hands-on works, such as this. Hampshire writes from her home in Lakewood, Ohio.

Learn more about John Deere's Lawn Care series and Hampshire's writing on www.kristenhampshire.com.

Photograper Credits

Dennis Anderson/Randall Whitehead Lighting Design/
www.randallwhitehead.com, 144; 145; 149

Courtesy of Creative Publishing international, 15; 16; 21;
22; 23; 24; 25; 30; 31; 33; 34; 42 (top); 55; 56; 58;
94; 106; 107; 108; 109; 123; 130; 131; 132; 138; 139;
140; 160; 161

Courtesy of John Deere, 7 (top); 60; 62; 65; 68; 69; 70;
71; 72; 73; 74; 75; 76 (top); 78; 79; 80; 81; 82: 83;
88; 89; 91; 92; 93; 96; 98; 99; 100; 101

Douglas Hope Hooper/Avalon Artistic Landscape
Lighting, 146

Courtesy of Hunter Industries, 5 (top); 44; 45; 124

iStockphoto, 7 (bottom); 8; 9; 35; 67; 152; 154; 156; 158;
159; 162; 167

Dency Kane, 26; 36; 38; 64; 111; 117; 119; 120 (top); 121
(bottom); 133 (bottom, left); 141

Dency Kane/Karen Fisher Design, 37; 128

Dency Kane/Carol Mercer & Lisa Verderosa, Design, 103

Douglas Keister/www.keisterphoto.com, 105; 121 (top);
129; 133 (top, right); 133 (bottom, right); 137; 143

Clive Nichols Garden Pictures/www.clivenichols.com, 84;
87; 95; 112; 113; 114; 118; 133 (top, left)

Allan Penn, 5 (bottom); 27; 42 (middle & bottom); 43; 52;
54; 59; 110; 115; 126; 127; 147; 148; 150; 151

Brian Vanden Brink, 17; 29; 50; 63; 134; 135

Brian Vanden Brink/Catalano Architects, 11; 49

Brian Vanden Brink/Green Company, Architects, 13

Brian Vanden Brink/Horiuchi & Solien Landscape
Architects, 7 (middle); 120 (bottom)

Brian Vanden Brink/Keith LeBlanc Landscape
Architecture, 6

Brian Vanden Brink/John Morris, Architect, 142

Brian Vanden Brink/Robinson and Grisaru Architects, 47

Index

traffic tolerance, 20

transitional zone, 19

transpiration, 38, 39

tree care specialists, 156–157

trees

    mowing around, 81

    trimming, 97–99

trimmers, 86, 88–93

trimming, 84–93

    vs. edging, 85

    shrubs, 94–96, 98

    timing, 86

    tools, 88–93

    trees, 97–99

tropical grasses, 15

turfgrass. See grass

Turfgrass Climate Zone Map, 18–19

two-cycle equipment, 90–93

U

uplighting, 149

V

verticutting, 108

voltage drop, 152

W

walk-behind mower, 68

warm/arid zone, 19

warm climate maintenance, 159

warm/humid zone, 18

warm-season grasses, 15, 54–55

water conservation, 46

water deprivation, 22–23

water-garden plants, 136, 141, 142

water/watering, 36–47

    even coverage, 46

    irrigation systems, 44–45

    need for, 38–39

    schedule, 41

    sprinklers, 42–43

    timing, 40–41

weed control products, 56–57

wildlife control, 162–165

wind, 46

winter maintenance, 159

wood edging, 113

Z

zero-turn mower, 70, 81

Zoysia grass, 78, 161

Notes